INTRODUCTION

This is a technical explanation of the Convention between the United States and Ireland and the Protocol signed on July 28, 1997 (the "Convention" and "Protocol"). References are made to the Convention between the Government of the United States of America and the Government of Ireland for the Avoidance of Double Taxation and the Prevention of Fiscal Evasion with Respect to Taxes on Income, signed on September 13, 1949 (the "prior Convention"). The Convention replaces the prior Convention.

In connection with the negotiation of the Convention and the Protocol, the negotiators developed and agreed upon an exchange of diplomatic notes. The notes constitute an agreement between the two governments which shall enter into force at the same time as the entry into force of the Convention. These understandings and interpretations are intended to give guidance both to the taxpayers and the tax authorities of both Contracting States in interpreting the relevant provisions of the Convention.

Negotiations took into account the U.S. Treasury Department's current tax treaty policy, the Model Income Tax Convention on Income and on Capital, published by the OECD in 1992 and amended in 1994 and 1995 (the "OECD Model") and recent tax treaties concluded by both countries. References to the "U.S. Model" refer to the U.S. Treasury Department's Model Income Tax Convention of September 20, 1996, which was issued after negotiation of the Convention was substantially completed, although prior drafts of the U.S. Model were available and taken into account in the course of negotiations.

The Technical Explanation is an official guide to the Convention and Protocol. It reflects the policies behind particular Convention provisions, as well as understandings reached with respect to the application and interpretation of the Convention and Protocol. In the discussions of each Article in this explanation, the relevant portions of the Protocol and notes are discussed. This Technical Explanation has been provided to Ireland. References in the Technical Explanation to "he" or "his" should be read to mean "he or she" and "his or her."

## Article 1 (General Scope)

*Paragraph 1*

Paragraph 1 of Article 1 provides that the Convention applies to residents of the United States or Ireland except where the terms of the Convention provide otherwise. Under Article 4 (Residence) a person is generally treated as a resident of a Contracting State if that person is, under the laws of that State, liable to tax therein by reason of his domicile or other similar criteria. If, however, a person is considered a resident of both Contracting States, a single state of residence generally is assigned under Article 4. This definition governs for all purposes of the Convention.

Certain provisions are applicable to persons who may not be residents of either Contracting State. For example, Article 19 (Government Service) may apply to an employee of a Contracting State who is resident in neither State. Paragraph 1 of Article 25 (Non-Discrimination) applies to nationals of the Contracting States. Under Article 27 (Exchange of Information and Administrative Assistance), information may be exchanged with respect to residents of third states.

*Paragraph 2*

Paragraph 2 states the generally accepted relationship both between the Convention and domestic law and between the Convention and other agreements between the Contracting States (i.e., that no provision in the Convention may restrict any exclusion, exemption, deduction, credit or other benefit accorded by the tax laws of the Contracting States, or by any other agreement between the Contracting States). For example, if a deduction would be allowed under the U.S. Internal Revenue Code (the "Code") in computing the U.S. taxable income of a resident of the Ireland, the deduction also is allowed to that person in computing taxable income under the Convention. Paragraph 2 also means that the Convention may not increase the tax burden on a resident of a Contracting States beyond the burden determined under domestic law. Thus, a right to tax given by the Convention cannot be exercised unless that right also exists under internal law. The relationship between the non-discrimination provisions of the Convention and other agreements is not addressed in paragraph 2 but in paragraph 3.

It follows that under the principle of paragraph 2 a taxpayer's liability to U.S. tax need not be determined under the Convention if the Code would produce a more favorable result. A taxpayer may not, however, choose among the provisions of the Code and the Convention in an inconsistent manner in order to minimize tax. For example, assume that a resident of the other Contracting State has three separate businesses in the United States. One is a profitable permanent establishment and the other two are trades or businesses that would earn taxable income under the Code but that do not meet the permanent establishment threshold tests of the Convention. One is profitable and the other incurs a loss. Under the Convention, the income of the permanent establishment is taxable, and both the profit and loss of the other two businesses are ignored. Under the Code, all three would be subject to tax, but the loss would be offset against the profits of the two profitable ventures. The taxpayer may not invoke the Convention to exclude the profits of the profitable trade or business and invoke the Code to claim the loss of the loss trade or business against the profit of the permanent establishment. (See Rev. Rul. 84-17, 1984-1 C.B. 308.) If, however, the taxpayer invokes the Code for the taxation of all three ventures, he would not be precluded from invoking the Convention with respect, for example, to any dividend income he may receive from the United States that is not effectively connected with any of his business activities in the United States.

Similarly, nothing in the Convention can be used to deny any benefit granted by any other agreement between the United States and Ireland. For example, if certain benefits were provided for military personnel or military contractors under a Status of Forces Agreement between the United States and Ireland, those benefits or protections would be available to residents of the Contracting States regardless of any provisions to the contrary (or silence) in the Convention.

*Paragraph 3*

Paragraph 3 specifically relates to non-discrimination obligations of the Contracting States under other agreements. The provisions of paragraph 3 are an exception to the rule provided in paragraph 2 of this Article under which the Convention shall not restrict in any manner any benefit now or hereafter accorded by any other agreement between the Contracting States.

Subparagraph (a)(i) of paragraph 3 provides that, notwithstanding any other agreement to which the Contracting States may be parties, a dispute concerning whether a measure is within the scope of this Convention shall be considered only by the competent authorities of the Contracting States, and the procedures under this Convention exclusively shall apply to the dispute. Thus, procedures for dealing with disputes that may be incorporated into trade, investment, or other agreements between the Contracting States shall not apply for the purpose of determining the scope of the Convention.

Subparagraph (a)(ii) of paragraph 3 provides that, unless the competent authorities determine that a taxation measure is not within the scope of this Convention, the nondiscrimination obligations of this Convention exclusively shall apply with respect to that measure, except for such national treatment or most-favored-nation ("MFN") obligations as may apply to trade in goods under the General Agreement on Tariffs and Trade ("GATT"). No national treatment or MFN obligation under any other agreement shall apply with respect to that measure. Thus, unless the competent authorities agree otherwise, any national treatment and MFN obligations undertaken by the Contracting States under agreements other than the Convention shall not apply to a taxation measure, with the exception of GATT as applicable to trade in goods.

Subparagraph (b) of paragraph 3 defines a "measure" broadly. It would include, for example, a law, regulation, rule, procedure, decision, administrative action or guidance, or any similar provision or action.

*Paragraph 4*

Paragraph 4 contains the traditional saving clause found in U.S. tax treaties. The Contracting States reserve their rights, except as provided in paragraph 5, to tax their residents and citizens as provided in their internal laws, notwithstanding any provisions of the Convention to the contrary. For example, if a resident of Ireland performs independent personal services in the United States and the income from the services is not attributable to a fixed base in the United States, Article 14 (Independent Personal Services) would by its terms prevent the United States from taxing the income. If, however, the resident of Ireland is also a citizen of the United States, the saving clause permits the United States to include the remuneration in the worldwide income of the citizen and subject it to tax under the normal Code rules (i.e., without regard to Code section 894(a)). For special foreign tax credit rules applicable to the U.S. taxation of certain U.S. income of its citizens resident in Ireland, see paragraph 3 of Article 24 (Relief from Double Taxation).

For purposes of the saving clause, "residence" is determined under Article 4 (Residence). Thus, if an individual who is not a U.S. citizen is a resident of the United States under the Code, and is also a resident of Ireland under its law, and that individual has a permanent home available to him in Ireland and not in the United States, he would be treated as a resident of Ireland under Article 4 and for purposes of the saving clause. The United States would not be permitted to apply its statutory rules to that person if they are inconsistent with the treaty. Thus, an individual who is a U.S. resident under the Internal Revenue Code but who is deemed to be a resident of Ireland under the tie-breaker rules of Article 4 (Residence) would be subject to U.S. tax only to the extent permitted by the Convention. However, the person would be treated as a U.S. resident for U.S. tax purposes other than determining the individual's U.S. tax liability. For example, in determining under Code section 957 whether a foreign corporation is a controlled foreign corporation, shares in that corporation held by the individual would be considered to be held by a U.S. resident. As a result, other U.S. citizens or residents might be deemed to be United States shareholders of a controlled foreign corporation subject to current inclusion of Subpart F income recognized by the corporation. See, Treas. Reg. section 301.7701(b)-7(a)(3).

Under paragraph 4 each Contracting State also reserves its right to tax former citizens whose loss of citizenship had as one of its principal purposes the avoidance of tax. The United States generally treats a former citizen as having a principal purpose to avoid tax if (a) the average annual net income tax of such individual for the period of 5 taxable years ending before the date of the loss of status is greater than $100,000, or (b) the net worth of such individual as of such date is $500,000 or more. In the United States, such a former citizen is taxable in accordance with the provisions of section 877 of the Code.

*Paragraph 5*

Some provisions are intended to provide benefits to citizens and residents even if they do not exist under internal law. Paragraph 5 sets forth certain exceptions to the saving clause that preserve these benefits for citizens and residents of the Contracting States. Subparagraph (a) lists certain provisions of the Convention that are applicable to all citizens and residents of a Contracting State, despite the general saving clause rule of paragraph 4: (1) Paragraph 2 of Article 9 (Associated Enterprises) provides for correlative adjustments with respect to income tax due on profits reallocated under Article 9. (2) Paragraph 2 of Article 16 (Directors' Fees) requires a Contracting State to treat certain directors' fees as arising in the other Contracting State, even if they would otherwise be treated as arising in the first-mentioned State. (3) Paragraphs 1(b) and 4 of Article 18 (Pensions, Social Security, Annuities, Alimony and Child Support) deal with social security benefits and child support payments, respectively. The inclusion of paragraph 1(b) in the exceptions to the saving clause means, for example, that the grant of exclusive taxing right of social security benefits to the residence country applies to deny to the United States the right to tax its citizens that are residents of Ireland on U.S. social security benefits. The inclusion of paragraph 4, which exempts child support payments from taxation by both Contracting States, means that if a resident of Ireland pays child support to a citizen or resident of the United States, the United States may not tax the recipient. (4) Article 24 (Relief from Double Taxation) confirms the benefit of a credit to citizens and residents of one Contracting State for income taxes paid to the other. (5) Article 25 (Non-Discrimination) requires one Contracting State to grant national treatment to residents and citizens of the other Contracting State in certain circumstances. Excepting this Article from the saving clause requires, for example, that the United States give such benefits to a resident or citizen of Ireland even if that person is a citizen of the United States. (6) Article 26 (Mutual Agreement Procedure) may confer benefits on citizens and residents of the Contracting States. For example, the statute of limitations may be waived for refunds and the competent authorities are permitted to use a definition of a term that differs from the internal law definition. As with the foreign tax credit, these benefits are intended to be granted by a Contracting State to its citizens and residents.

Subparagraph (b) of paragraph 5 provides a different set of exceptions to the saving clause. The benefits referred to are all intended to be granted to temporary residents of a Contracting State (for example, in the case of the United States, holders of non-immigrant visas), but not to citizens or to persons who have acquired permanent residence in that State. If beneficiaries of these provisions travel from one of the Contracting States to the other, and remain in the other long enough to become residents under its internal law, but do not acquire permanent residence status (i.e., in the U.S. context, they do not become "green card" holders) and are not citizens of that State, the host State will continue to grant these benefits even if they conflict with the statutory rules. The benefits preserved by this paragraph are the tax treatment of pension fund contributions under paragraph 5 of Article 18 (Pensions, Social Security, Annuities, Alimony, and Child Support), and the host country exemptions for the following items of income: government service salaries and pensions under Article 19 (Government Service); certain income of visiting students and trainees under Article 20 (Students and Trainees); and the income of diplomatic agents and consular officers under Article 28 (Diplomatic Agents and Consular Officers).

### Article 2 (Taxes Covered)

This Article specifies the U.S. taxes and the taxes of Ireland to which the Convention applies. Unlike Article 2 in the OECD Model, this Article does not contain a general description of the types of taxes that are covered (i.e., income taxes), but only a listing of the specific taxes covered for both of the Contracting States. The taxes specified in Article 2 are the covered taxes for all purposes of the Convention. In most U.S. treaties and the U.S. Model, the non-discrimination and information exchange provisions apply to a broader class of taxes, including state and local taxes in the case of non-discrimination. The Convention does not do so, however, because of restrictions in Irish law.

*Paragraph 1*

Subparagraph 1(a) provides that the United States covered taxes are the Federal income taxes imposed by the Code, except the accumulated earnings tax and personal holding company tax (which are considered penalty taxes), and the excise taxes imposed on insurance premiums paid to foreign insurers (Code section 4371), and with respect to private foundations (Code sections 4940 through 4948). Although they may be regarded as income taxes, social security taxes (Code sections 1401, 3101, 3111 and 3301) are specifically excluded from coverage. Income taxes on social security benefits are covered, however, and are dealt with in subparagraph 1(b) of Article 18 (Pensions, Social Security, Annuities, Alimony and Child Support). U.S. and Irish social security taxes are dealt with in the bilateral Social Security Totalization Agreement, which entered into force on September 1, 1993. State and local taxes in the United States are not covered by the Convention.

The Convention applies to the federal excise tax on insurance premiums only to the extent that the risks covered by such premiums are not reinsured, directly or indirectly, with a person not entitled (under this or any other convention to which the United States is a party) to exemption from the tax and, under paragraph 2 of the Protocol, only to the extent that the premiums are subject to the generally applicable tax imposed on insurance companies in the Contracting State in which the insurers are resident. Accordingly, if a company is entitled to benefits under a special tax regime under the laws of a Contracting State that provides for a rate of tax lower than the normal corporate rate of tax, it would not qualify for benefits with respect to the FET.

To the extent the Convention provides coverage for the U.S. insurance excise tax, it effectively exempts from the tax Irish companies that insure U.S. risks, subject to the anti-conduit rule for reinsurance described above. Under the Code, the tax applies only to premiums that are not effectively connected to an active trade or business in the United States or that are exempt by treaty from net basis U.S. income tax (because they are not attributable to a permanent establishment). Under Article 7 (Business Profits), the United States does not subject the business profits of an Irish enterprise to a tax that is covered by the Convention if the income of the enterprise is not attributable to a permanent establishment that the enterprise has in the United States. In contrast with this Convention, the prior Convention did not cover the insurance excise tax, allowing it to be imposed on premiums paid to Irish insurers if such premiums were not attributable to a permanent establishment of the insurer in the United States.

Subparagraph 1(b) provides that the Irish covered taxes are the income tax, the corporation tax and the capital gains tax.

*Paragraph 2*

Under paragraph 2, the Convention will apply to any taxes that are identical, or substantially similar, to those enumerated in paragraph 1, and which are imposed in addition to, or in place of, the existing taxes after the date of signature of the Convention. The paragraph also provides that the competent authorities of the Contracting States will notify each other of significant changes in their taxation laws. The use of the term "significant" means that changes must be reported that are of significance to the operation of the Convention.

The competent authorities are also obligated to notify each other of official published materials concerning the application of the Convention. This requirement encompasses materials such as technical explanations, regulations, rulings and judicial decisions relating to the Convention.

### Article 3 (General Definitions)

Paragraph 1 defines a number of basic terms used in the Convention. Certain others are defined in other articles of the Convention. For example, the term "resident of a Contracting State" is defined in Article 4 (Residence). The term "permanent establishment" is defined in Article 5 (Permanent Establishment). The terms "dividends," "interest" and "royalties" are defined in Articles 10, 11 and 12, respectively. The introduction to paragraph 1 makes clear that these definitions apply for all purposes of the Convention, unless the context requires otherwise. This latter condition allows flexibility in the interpretation of the treaty in order to avoid unintended results. Terms that are not defined in the Convention are dealt with in paragraph 2.

*Paragraph 1*

Subparagraph 1(a) defines the term "person" to include an individual, an estate, a trust, a partnership, a company and any other body of persons. The definition is significant for a variety of reasons. For example, subparagraph 1(a) of Article 4 treats only a "person" as a "resident" that can qualify for most benefits under the treaty. Also, all "persons" are eligible to claim relief under Article 26 (Mutual Agreement Procedure).

This definition corresponds to the definition in the U.S. Model, which is more specific but not substantively different from the corresponding provision in the OECD Model. Unlike the OECD Model, it specifically includes an estate, a trust, and a partnership. Since, however, the OECD Model's definition also uses the phrase "and any other body of persons," partnerships would be included, consistent with paragraph 2 of the Article, to the extent that they are treated as "bodies of persons" under the law of the Contracting State making the determination. Furthermore, because the OECD Model uses the term "includes," trusts and estates would be persons. Under paragraph 2, the meaning of the terms "partnership," "trust" and "estate" would be determined by reference to the law of the Contracting State whose tax is being applied.

The term "company" is defined in subparagraph 1(b) as a body corporate or an entity treated as a body corporate for tax purposes. Although the Convention does not add "in the state in which it is organized," as does the U.S. Model, the result should be the same, as the Commentaries to the OECD Model interprets language identical to that of the Convention in a manner consistent with the U.S. Model.

The terms "enterprise of a Contracting State" and "enterprise of the other Contracting State" are defined in subparagraph 1(c) as an enterprise carried on by a resident of a Contracting State and an enterprise carried on by a resident of the other Contracting State. The term "enterprise" is not defined in the Convention, nor is it defined in the U.S. Model or the OECD Model or its Commentaries. Despite the absence of a clear, generally accepted meaning for the term "enterprise," the term is understood to refer to any activity or set of activities that constitutes a trade or business.

An enterprise of a Contracting State need not be carried on in that State. It may be carried on in the other Contracting State or a third state (e.g., a U.S. corporation doing all of its business in Ireland would still be a U.S. enterprise).

Subparagraph 1(d) defines the term "international traffic." The term means any transport by a ship or aircraft except when the vessel is operated solely between places within a Contracting State. This definition is applicable principally in the context of Article 8 (Shipping and Air Transport). The definition in the OECD Model refers to the operator of the ship or aircraft having its place of effective management in a Contracting State (i.e., being a resident of that State). The Convention, like the U.S. Model, does not include this limitation. The broader definition combines with paragraphs 2 and 3 of Article 8 to exempt from tax by the source State income from the rental of ships, aircraft or containers that is earned both by lessors that are operators of ships and aircraft and by those lessors that are not (e.g., a bank or a container leasing company).

The exclusion from international traffic of transport solely between places within a Contracting State means, for example, that carriage of goods or passengers solely between New York and Chicago would not be treated as international traffic, whether carried by a U.S. or a foreign carrier. The substantive taxing rules of the Convention relating to the taxation of income from transport, principally Article 8 (Shipping and Air Transport), therefore, would not apply to income from such carriage. Thus, if the carrier engaged in internal U.S. traffic were a resident of Ireland (assuming that were possible under U.S. law), the United States would not be required to exempt the income from that transport under Article 8. The income would, however, be treated as business profits under Article 7 (Business Profits), and therefore would be taxable in the United States only if attributable to a U.S. permanent establishment of the foreign carrier, and then only on a net basis. The gross basis U.S. tax imposed by section 887 would never apply under the circumstances described. If, however, goods or passengers are carried by a carrier resident in Ireland from a non-U.S. port to, for example, New York, and some of the goods or passengers continue on to Chicago, the entire transport would be international traffic. This would be true if the international carrier transferred the goods at the U.S. port of entry from a ship to a land vehicle, from a ship to a lighter, or even if the overland portion of the trip in the United States was handled by an independent carrier under contract with the original international carrier, so long as both parts of the trip were reflected in original bills of lading. For this reason, the Convention, like the U.S. Model refers, in the definition of "international traffic," to "such transport" being solely between places in the other Contracting State, while the OECD Model refers to the ship or aircraft being operated solely between such places. The Convention definition is intended to make clear that, as in the above example, even if the goods are carried on a different aircraft for the internal portion of the international voyage than is used for the overseas portion of the trip, the definition applies to that internal portion as well as the external portion.

Finally, a "cruise to nowhere," i.e., a cruise beginning and ending in a port in the same Contracting State with no stops in a foreign port, would not constitute international traffic.

Subparagraphs 1(e)(i) and (ii) define the term "competent authority" for the United States and Ireland, respectively. The U.S. competent authority is the Secretary of the Treasury or his delegate. The Secretary of the Treasury has delegated the competent authority function to the Commissioner of Internal Revenue, who in turn has delegated the authority to the Assistant Commissioner (International). With respect to interpretative issues, the Assistant Commissioner acts with the concurrence of the Associate Chief Counsel (International) of the Internal Revenue Service.

The term "United States" is defined in subparagraph 1(f) to mean the United States of America, including the states, the District of Columbia and the territorial sea of the United States. The term does not include Puerto Rico, the Virgin Islands, Guam or any other U.S. possession or territory. The term also explicitly includes certain areas under the sea within the definition of the United States. For certain purposes, the definition is extended to include the sea bed and subsoil of undersea areas adjacent to the territorial sea of the United States. This extension applies to the extent that the United States exercises sovereignty in accordance with international law for the purpose of natural resource exploration and exploitation of such areas.

The definition of United States produces results consistent with the result that would be obtained under the sometimes less precise definitions in some U.S. treaties. In the absence of a precise definition incorporating the continental shelf, the term "United States of America" would be interpreted by reference to the U.S. internal law definition. Section 638 treats the continental shelf as part of the United States.

The term "Ireland" is defined in subparagraph 1(g) and also includes the sea bed in circumstances similar to those in which the sea bed will be considered part of the United States..

Subparagraph 1(h) defines the term "Contracting States" as Ireland and the United States. The terms "Contracting State," "one of the Contracting States" and "the other Contracting State" mean Ireland <u>or</u> the United States, as the context requires.

The term "national," as it relates to the United States and to Ireland, is defined in subparagraphs 1(i). This term is relevant for purposes of Articles 19 (Government Service) and 24 (Non-Discrimination). A national of one of the Contracting States is (1) an individual who is a citizen of that State, and (2) any legal person, association or other entity deriving its status as such from the law in force in that Contracting State. This definition is closely analogous to that found in the U.S. and OECD Models.

The inclusion of juridical persons in the definition may have significance in relation to paragraph 1 of Article 25 (Non-Discrimination), which provides that nationals of one Contracting State may not be subject in the other to any taxes or connected requirements that are other or more burdensome than those applicable to nationals of that other State who are in the same circumstances.

The Convention includes a defined term, "qualified governmental entity," found in the U.S. but not the OECD Model. This definition, found in subparagraph 1(j), is relevant for purposes of Articles 4 (Residence) and 22 (Limitation on Benefits). The term means: (i) the Government of a Contracting State or of a political subdivision or local authority of the Contracting State; (ii) A person wholly owned, directly or indirectly, by a governmental entity described in subparagraph (i), that satisfies certain organizational and funding standards; and (iii) a pension fund that meets the standards of subparagraphs (i) and (ii) that is constituted and operated exclusively to administer or provide government service pension benefits described in Article 19 (Government Service). A qualified governmental entity may not engage in any commercial activity.

*Paragraph 2*

Paragraph 2 provides that in the application of the Convention, any term used but not defined in the Convention will have the meaning that it has under the law of the Contracting State whose tax is being applied, unless the context requires otherwise. In general, if a term is defined under both the tax and non-tax laws of a Contracting State, the definition in the tax law will take precedence over the definition in the non-tax laws. Finally, there also may be cases where the tax laws of a State contain multiple definitions of the same term. In such a case, the definition used for purposes of the particular provision at issue, if any, should be used.

If the meaning of a term cannot be readily determined under the law of a Contracting State, or if there is a conflict in meaning under the laws of the two States that creates difficulties in the application of the Convention, the competent authorities, as indicated in paragraph 3(f) of Article 26 (Mutual Agreement Procedure), may establish a common meaning in order to prevent double taxation or to further any other purpose of the Convention. This common meaning need not conform to the meaning of the term under the laws of either Contracting State.

Like the U.S. Model, the Convention clarifies that the reference in paragraph 2 to the internal law of a Contracting State means the law in effect at the time the treaty is being applied, not the law as in effect at the time the treaty was signed. This use of "ambulatory definitions" is understood to have been implicit in the OECD Model.

The use of an ambulatory definition, however, may lead to results that are at variance with the intentions of the negotiators and of the Contracting States when the treaty was negotiated and ratified. The reference in both paragraphs 1 and 2 to the "context otherwise requiring" a definition different from the treaty definition, in paragraph 1, or from the internal law definition of the Contracting State whose tax is being imposed, under paragraph 2, refers to a circumstance where the result intended by the negotiators or by the Contracting States is different from the result that would obtain under either the paragraph 1 definition or the statutory definition. Thus, flexibility in defining terms is necessary and permitted.

## Article 4 (Residence)

This Article sets forth rules for determining whether a person is a resident of a Contracting State for purposes of the Convention. As a general matter only residents of the Contracting States may claim the benefits of the Convention. The treaty definition of residence is to be used only for purposes of the Convention. The fact that a person is determined to be a resident of a Contracting State under Article 4 does not necessarily entitle that person to the benefits of the Convention. In addition to being a resident, a person also must qualify for benefits under Article 23 (Limitation on Benefits) in order to receive benefits conferred on residents of a Contracting State.

The determination of residence for treaty purposes looks first to a person's liability to tax as a resident under the respective taxation laws of the Contracting States. As a general matter, a person who, under those laws, is a resident of one Contracting State and not of the other need look no further. That person is a resident for purposes of the Convention of the State in which he is resident under internal law. If, however, a person is resident in both Contracting States under their respective taxation laws, the Article proceeds, where possible, to assign a single State of residence to such a person for purposes of the Convention through the use of tie-breaker rules.

*Paragraph 1*

The term "resident of a Contracting State" is defined in paragraph 1. Subparagraph (a) incorporates the definitions of residence in U.S. and Irish law by referring to a resident as a person who, under the laws of a Contracting State, is subject to tax there by reason of his domicile, residence, place of management, place of incorporation or any other similar criterion. Thus, residents of the United States include aliens who are considered U.S. residents under Code section 7701(b) unless the alien is a "green card" holder not described in the second sentence of subparagraph (a). Subparagraphs (b) through (d) each address special cases that may arise in the context of Article 4.

Subparagraph 1(a) specifically provides that a U.S. citizen would generally be treated as a resident of the United States. However, subparagraph (a) also provides that a U.S. citizen or alien lawfully admitted for permanent residence (i.e., a "green card" holder) will be treated as a resident of the United States for purposes of the Convention, and, thereby entitled to treaty benefits, only if he has a substantial presence (see section 7701(b)(3)), permanent home or habitual abode in the United States. If, however, such an individual is a resident both of the United States and Ireland under the general rule of paragraph 1(a), whether he is to be treated as a resident of the United States or of Ireland for purposes of the Convention is determined by the tie-breaker rules of paragraph 3 of the Article, regardless of how close his nexus to the United States may be. However, the fact that a U.S. citizen who does not have close ties to the United States may not be treated as a U.S. resident under the Convention does not alter the application of the saving clause of paragraph 4 of Article 1 (General Scope) to that citizen. For example, a U.S. citizen who pursuant to the "citizen/green card holder" rule is not considered to be a resident of the United States still is taxable on his worldwide income under the generally applicable rules of the Code.

Certain entities that are nominally subject to tax but that in practice rarely pay tax also would generally be treated as residents and therefore accorded treaty benefits. For example, RICs, REITs and REMICs are all residents of the United States for purposes of the treaty. Although the income earned by these entities normally is not subject to U.S. tax in the hands of the entity, they are taxable to the extent that they do not currently distribute their profits, and therefore may be regarded as "liable to tax." They also must satisfy a number of requirements under the Code in order to be entitled to special tax treatment.

Subparagraph (b) specifies that a qualified governmental entity (as defined in Article 3) of a State is to be treated as a resident of that State. Although this provision is not contained in some U.S. treaties, it is generally understood that such entities are to be treated as residents under all of those treaties. The purpose of including the rule in the Convention, and in the new U.S. Model, is to make this understanding explicit. Article 4 of the OECD Model was amended in 1995 to adopt a similar approach.

Subparagraph (c) provides that certain tax-exempt entities such as pension funds and charitable organizations will be regarded as residents regardless of whether they are generally liable for income tax in the State where they are established. A pension fund established in a Contracting State will be described in this subparagraph if it is established or sponsored by a person who is otherwise a resident under Article 4 and it is maintained to administer or provide retirement or employee benefits, such as health and disability benefits. A charitable or other exempt organization is a resident if the use of the organization's assets is limited to the accomplishment of the purposes serving as the basis for the exemption from tax.

The inclusion of this provision is intended to clarify the generally accepted practice of treating an entity that would be liable for tax as a resident under the internal law of a state but for a specific exemption from tax (either complete or partial) as a resident of that state for purposes of paragraph 1. Thus, a U.S. pension trust, or an exempt section 501(c) organization (such as a U.S. charity) that is generally exempt from tax under U.S. law is considered a resident of the United States for all purposes of the treaty.

Subparagraph (d) clarifies that certain investment vehicles are residents of the Contracting States in which they are created or organized, even though the tax on the income they derive may be imposed only or primarily at the level of their shareholders, beneficiaries, or owners. Specific examples of this category given in the Convention include U.S. regulated investment companies, real estate investment trusts and Irish Collective Investment Undertakings; the competent authorities may extend this treatment to additional investment entities.

Paragraph 1 of the Protocol addresses special problems presented by fiscally transparent entities such as partnerships and certain estates and trusts that are not subject to tax at the entity level. This subparagraph applies to any resident of a Contracting State who is entitled to income derived through an entity that is treated as fiscally transparent under the laws of either Contracting State. Entities falling under this description in the United States would include partnerships, common investment trusts under section 584 and grantor trusts. This paragraph also applies to U.S. limited liability companies ("LLC's") that are treated as partnerships for U.S. tax purposes.

Paragraph 1 of the Protocol provides that an item of income derived by such a fiscally transparent entity will be considered to be derived by a resident of a Contracting State if the resident is treated under the taxation laws of the State where he is resident as deriving the item of income. For example, if an Irish corporation distributes a dividend to an entity that is treated as fiscally transparent for U.S. tax purposes, the dividend will be considered derived by a resident of the United States only to the extent that the taxation laws of the United States treat one or more U.S. residents (whose status as U.S. residents is determined, for this purpose, under U.S. tax laws) as deriving the dividend income for U.S. tax purposes. In the case of a partnership, the persons who are, under U.S. tax laws, treated as partners of the entity would normally be the persons whom the U.S. tax laws would treat as deriving the dividend income through the partnership. Thus, it also follows that persons whom the U.S. treats as partners but who are not U.S. residents for U.S. tax purposes may not claim a benefit for the dividend paid to the entity under the U.S.-Ireland Convention. Although these partners are treated as deriving the income for U.S. tax purposes, they are not residents of the United States for purposes of the treaty. If, however, the country in which they are treated as resident for tax purposes (as determined under the laws of that country) has an income tax convention with Ireland, they may be entitled to claim a benefit under that convention. In contrast, if an entity is organized under U.S. laws and is classified as a corporation for U.S. tax purposes, dividends paid by an Irish corporation to the U.S. entity will be considered derived by a resident of the United States since the U.S. corporation is treated under U.S. taxation laws as a resident of the United States and as deriving the income.

These results would obtain even if the entity were viewed differently under the tax laws of Ireland (e.g., as not fiscally transparent in the first example above where the entity is treated as a partnership for U.S. tax purposes or as fiscally transparent in the second example where the entity is viewed as not fiscally transparent for U.S. tax purposes). These results also follow regardless of where the entity is organized, i.e., in the United States, in Ireland, or in a third country. For example, income from Irish sources received by an entity organized under the laws of Ireland, which is treated for U.S. tax purposes as a corporation and is owned by a U.S. shareholder who is a U.S. resident for U.S. tax purposes, is not considered derived by the shareholder of that corporation even if, under the tax laws of Ireland, the entity is treated as fiscally transparent. Rather, for purposes of the Convention, the income is treated as derived by the Irish entity. These results also follow regardless of whether the entity is disregarded as a separate entity under the laws of one jurisdiction but not the other, such as a single owner entity that is viewed as a branch for U.S. tax purposes and as a corporation for Irish tax purposes.

This rule also applies to trusts to the extent that they are fiscally transparent in either Contracting State. For example, if X, a resident of Ireland, creates a revocable trust with the trustee in a third country and names persons resident in a third country as the beneficiaries of the trust, X would be treated as the beneficial owner of income derived from the United States under the Code's rules. However, if the income is not taxed in Ireland, either because Ireland has no rules comparable to those in sections 671 through 679 or because the trustee is not an Irish resident, then, under paragraph 1 of the Protocol, the trust's income would not be regarded as being derived by a resident of Ireland.

The taxation laws of a Contracting State may treat an item of income, profit or gain as income, profit or gain of a resident of that State even if the resident is not subject to tax on that particular item of income, profit or gain.  For example, even though Ireland exempts certain dividends derived by an Irish parent corporation from Irish taxation, such income would be regarded as income of a resident of Ireland who otherwise derived the income for purposes of applying Article 10 (Dividends) of the Convention.

*Paragraph 2*

Paragraph 2 provides that a person who is liable to tax in a Contracting State only in respect of income from sources within that State or of profits attributable to a permanent establishment in that State will not be treated as a resident of that Contracting State for purposes of the Convention.  Thus, a consular official of Ireland who is posted in the United States, who may be subject to U.S. tax on U.S. source investment income, but is not taxable in the United States on non-U.S. source income under a consular convention, would not be considered a resident of the United States for purposes of the Convention.  (See Code section 7701(b)(5)(B)).  Similarly, an enterprise of Ireland with a permanent establishment in the United States is not, by virtue of that permanent establishment, a resident of the United States.  The enterprise generally is subject to U.S. tax only with respect to its income that is attributable to the U.S. permanent establishment, not with respect to its worldwide income, as is a U.S. resident.

*Paragraph 3*

If, under the laws of the two Contracting States, and, thus, under paragraph 1, an individual is deemed to be a resident of both Contracting States, a series of tie-breaker rules are provided in paragraph 3 to determine a single State of residence for that individual.  These tests are to be applied in the order in which they are stated.  The first test is based on where the individual has a permanent home.  If that test is inconclusive because the individual has a permanent home available to him in both States, he will be considered to be a resident of the Contracting State where his personal and economic relations are closest (i.e., the location of his "center of vital interests").  If that test is also inconclusive, or if he does not have a permanent home available to him in either State, he will be treated as a resident of the Contracting State where he maintains an habitual abode.  If he has an habitual abode in both States or in neither of them, he will be treated as a resident of his Contracting State of citizenship.  If he is a citizen of both States or of neither, the matter will be considered by the competent authorities, who will attempt to agree on a single State of residence.

*Paragraph 4*

Paragraph 4 seeks to settle dual-residence issues for persons other than individuals (such as companies, trusts or estates).  A company is treated as resident in the United States if it is created or organized under the laws of the United States or a political subdivision.  If the same test were used to determine corporate residence under Irish law, dual corporate residence could not occur.  However, under Irish law, a corporation is treated as a resident of Ireland if its place of central management and control is there.  Dual residence, therefore, can arise if a corporation organized in the United States is managed in Ireland.  Paragraph 4 provides that, if a company is resident in both the United States and Ireland under paragraph 1,  the competent authorities shall endeavor to agree on one State of residence for purposes of the Convention.

## Article 5 (Permanent Establishment)

This Article defines the term "permanent establishment," a term that is significant for several articles of the Convention.  The existence of a permanent establishment in a Contracting State is necessary under Article 7 (Business Profits) for the taxation by that State of the business profits of a resident of the other Contracting State.  Since the term "fixed base" in Article 14 (Independent Personal Services) is understood by reference to the definition of "permanent establishment," this Article is also relevant for purposes of Article 14.  Articles 10, 11 and 12 (dealing with dividends, interest, and royalties, respectively) provide for reduced rates of tax at source on payments of these items of income to a resident of the other State only when the income is not attributable to a permanent establishment or fixed base that the recipient has in the source State.  The concept is also relevant in determining which Contracting State may tax certain gains under Article 13 (Capital Gains) and certain "other income" under Article 22 (Other Income).

The Article follows closely both the U.S. and OECD Models.  It does not differ significantly from the definition of a permanent establishment in the prior Convention.

*Paragraph 1*

The basic definition of the term "permanent establishment" is contained in paragraph 1.  As used in the Convention, the term means a fixed place of business through which the business of an enterprise is wholly or partly carried on.

*Paragraph 2*

Paragraph 2 lists a number of types of fixed places of business that constitute a permanent establishment.  This list is illustrative and non-exclusive.  According to paragraph 2, the term permanent establishment includes a place of management, a branch, an office, a factory, a workshop, and a mine, oil or gas well, quarry or other place of extraction of natural resources.  As indicated in the OECD Commentaries (see paragraphs 4 through 8), a general principle to be observed in determining whether a permanent establishment exists is that the place of business must be "fixed" in the sense that a particular building or physical location is used by the enterprise for the conduct of its business, and that it must be foreseeable that the enterprise's use of this building or other physical location will be more than temporary.

*Paragraph 3*

Paragraph 3 provides rules to determine whether a building site or a construction or installation project constitutes a permanent establishment for the contractor, or installer, etc. An activity is merely preparatory and does not create a permanent establishment under paragraph 4(e) unless the site, project, etc. lasts or continues for more than twelve months. This provision differs from the U.S. Model in that it does not cover offshore drilling rigs. Special rules regarding exploration and exploitation of natural resources are found in Article 21 (Offshore Exploration and Exploitation Activities).

The twelve-month test applies separately to each site or project. The twelve-month period begins when work (including preparatory work carried on by the enterprise) physically begins in a Contracting State. A series of contracts or projects by a contractor that are interdependent both commercially and geographically are to be treated as a single project for purposes of applying the twelve-month threshold test. For example, the construction of a housing development would be considered as a single project even if each house were constructed for a different purchaser.

If the twelve-month threshold is exceeded, the site or project constitutes a permanent establishment from the first day of activity. In applying this paragraph, time spent by a sub-contractor on a building site is counted as time spent by the general contractor at the site for purposes of determining whether the general contractor has a permanent establishment. However, for the sub-contractor itself to be treated as having a permanent establishment, the sub-contractor's activities at the site must last for more than 12 months. If a sub-contractor is on a site intermittently time is measured from the first day the sub-contractor is on the site until the last day (i.e., intervening days that the sub-contractor is not on the site are counted) for purposes of applying the 12-month rule.

These interpretations of the Article are based on the Commentary to paragraph 3 of Article 5 of the OECD Model, which contains language almost identical to that in the Convention. These interpretations are consistent with the generally accepted international interpretation of the language in paragraph 3 of Article 5 of the Convention.

*Paragraph 4*

Paragraph 4 contains exceptions to the general rule of paragraph 1, listing a number of activities that may be carried on through a fixed place of business, but which nevertheless do not create a permanent establishment. The use of facilities solely to store, display or deliver merchandise belonging to an enterprise does not constitute a permanent establishment of that enterprise. The maintenance of a stock of goods belonging to an enterprise solely for the purpose of storage, display or delivery, or solely for the purpose of processing by another enterprise does not give rise to a permanent establishment of the first-mentioned enterprise. The maintenance of a fixed place of business solely for the purpose of purchasing goods or merchandise, or for collecting information, for the enterprise, or for other activities that have a preparatory or auxiliary character for the enterprise, such as advertising, or the supply of information do not constitute a permanent establishment of the enterprise. Thus, as explained in paragraph 22 of the

OECD Commentaries, an employee of a news organization engaged merely in gathering information would not constitute a permanent establishment of the news organization.

Finally, subparagraph 4(f) provides that a combination of the activities described in the other subparagraphs of paragraph 4 will not give rise to a permanent establishment if the combination results in an overall activity that is of a preparatory or auxiliary character. This combination rule differs from that in the U.S. Model. In the U.S. Model, any combination of otherwise excepted activities is deemed not to give rise to a permanent establishment, without the additional requirement that the combination, as distinct from each constituent activity, be preparatory or auxiliary. It is assumed that if preparatory or auxiliary activities are combined, the combination generally will also be of a character that is preparatory or auxiliary. If, however, this is not the case, a permanent establishment may result from a combination of activities.

*Paragraph 5*

Paragraphs 5 and 6 specify when activities carried on by an agent on behalf of an enterprise create a permanent establishment of that enterprise. Under paragraph 5, a dependent agent of an enterprise is deemed to be a permanent establishment of the enterprise if the agent has and habitually exercises an authority to conclude contracts that are binding on the enterprise. If, however, the agent's activities are limited to those activities specified in paragraph 4 which would not constitute a permanent establishment if carried on by the enterprise through a fixed place of business, the agent is not a permanent establishment of the enterprise.

Like the OECD Model, the Convention uses the term "in the name of that enterprise," rather than the term "binding on the enterprise," found in the U.S. Model. As indicated in paragraph 32 to the OECD Commentaries on Article 5, paragraph 5 of the Article is intended to encompass persons who have "sufficient authority to bind the enterprise's participation in the business activity in the State concerned." Therefore, the change to the U.S. Model is merely a clarification and does not result in a substantive difference between the two provisions.

The contracts referred to in paragraph 5 are those relating to the essential business operations of the enterprise, rather than ancillary activities. For example, if the agent has no authority to conclude contracts in the name of the enterprise with its customers for, say, the sale of the goods produced by the enterprise, but it can enter into service contracts in the name of the enterprise for the enterprise's business equipment used in the agent's office, this contracting authority would not fall within the scope of the paragraph, even if exercised regularly.

*Paragraph 6*

Under paragraph 6, an enterprise is not deemed to have a permanent establishment in a Contracting State merely because it carries on business in that State through an independent agent, including a broker or general commission agent, if the agent is acting in the ordinary course of his business as an independent agent. Thus, there are two conditions that must be satisfied: the agent must be both legally and economically independent of the enterprise, and the agent must be acting in the ordinary course of its business in carrying out activities on behalf of the enterprise.

Whether the agent and the enterprise are independent is a factual determination. Among the questions to be considered are the extent to which the agent operates on the basis of instructions from the enterprise. An agent that is subject to detailed instructions regarding the conduct of its operations or comprehensive control by the enterprise is not legally independent.

In determining whether the agent is economically independent, a relevant factor is the extent to which the agent bears business risk. Business risk refers primarily to risk of loss. An independent agent typically bears risk of loss from its own activities. In the absence of other factors that would establish dependence, an agent that shares business risk with the enterprise, or has its own business risk, is economically independent because its business activities are not integrated with those of the principal. Conversely, an agent that bears little or no risk from the activities it performs is not economically independent and therefore is not described in paragraph 6.

Another relevant factor in determining whether an agent is economically independent is whether the agent has an exclusive or nearly exclusive relationship with the principal. Such a relationship may indicate that the principal has economic control over the agent. A number of principals acting in concert also may have economic control over an agent. The limited scope of the agent's activities and the agent's dependence on a single source of income may indicate that the agent lacks economic independence. It should be borne in mind, however, that exclusivity is not in itself a conclusive test: an agent may be economically independent notwithstanding an exclusive relationship with the principal if it has the capacity to diversify and acquire other clients without substantial modifications to its current business and without substantial harm to its business profits. Thus, exclusivity should be viewed merely as a pointer to further investigation of the relationship between the principal and the agent. Each case must be addressed on the basis of its own facts and circumstances.

*Paragraph 7*

Paragraph 7 clarifies that a company that is a resident of a Contracting State is not deemed to have a permanent establishment in the other Contracting State merely because it controls, or is controlled by, a company that is a resident of that other Contracting State, or that carries on business in that other Contracting State. The determination whether a permanent establishment exists is made solely on the basis of the factors described in paragraphs 1 through 6 of the Article. Whether a company is a permanent establishment of a related company, therefore, is based solely on those factors and not on the ownership or control relationship between the companies.

**Article 6 (Income from Immovable Property (Real Property))**

*Paragraph 1*

The first paragraph of Article 6 states the general rule that income of a resident of a Contracting State derived from immovable property (real property) situated in the other Contracting State may be taxed in the Contracting State in which the property is situated. The paragraph specifies that income from real property includes income from agriculture and forestry as in the U.S. and OECD Models. Given the availability of the net election in paragraph 3 of the Protocol, taxpayers generally should be able to obtain the same tax treatment in the situs country regardless of whether the income is treated as business profits or real property income. Paragraph 3 clarifies that the income referred to in paragraph 1 also means income from any use of real property, including, but not limited to, income from direct use by the owner (in which case income may be imputed to the owner for tax purposes) and rental income from the letting of real property.

This Article does not grant an exclusive taxing right to the situs State; the situs State is merely given the primary right to tax. The Article does not impose any limitation in terms of rate or form of tax on the situs State, except that, as provided in paragraph 3 of the Protocol, the situs State must allow the taxpayer an election to be taxed on a net basis. Under that provision, a resident of one Contracting State that derives real property income from the other may elect, for any taxable year, to be subject to tax in that other State on a net basis, as though the income were attributable to a permanent establishment in that other State. The election may be terminated with the consent of the competent authority of the situs State. In the United States, revocation will be granted in accordance with the provisions of Treas. Reg. section 1.871-10(d)(2).

*Paragraph 2*

The term "immovable property (real property)" is defined in paragraph 2 by reference to the internal law definition in the situs State. It is to be understood from the parenthetical use of the term "real property" in the title to the Article and in paragraphs 1 and 2 that the term is synonymous with the term "immovable property" which is used in the OECD Model and by many other countries. In the case of the United States, the term has the meaning given to it by Reg. § 1.897-1(b).

*Paragraph 3*

Paragraph 3 makes clear that all forms of income derived from the exploitation of real property are taxable in the Contracting State in which the property is situated. In the case of a net lease of real property, if a net election has not been made, the gross rental payment (before deductible expenses incurred by the lessee) is treated as income from the property. Income from the disposition of an interest in real property, however, is not considered "derived" from real property and is not dealt with in this article. The taxation of that income is addressed in Article 13 (Capital Gains). Also, the interest paid on a mortgage on real property and distributions by a U.S. Real Estate Investment Trust are not dealt with in Article 6. Such payments would fall under Articles 10 (Dividends), 11 (Interest) or 13 (Capital Gains). Finally, dividends paid by a United States Real Property Holding Corporation are not considered to be income from the exploitation of real property: such payments would fall under Article 10 (Dividends) or 13 (Capital Gains).

*Paragraph 4*

Paragraph 4 specifies that the basic rule of paragraph 1 (as elaborated in paragraph 3) applies to income from real property of an enterprise and to income from real property used for the performance of independent personal services. This clarifies that the situs country may tax the real property income (including rental income) of a resident of the other Contracting State in the absence of attribution to a permanent establishment or fixed base in the situs State. This provision represents an exception to the general rule under Articles 7 (Business Profits) and 14 (Independent Personal Services) that income must be attributable to a permanent establishment or fixed base, respectively, in order to be taxable in the situs state.

## Article 7 (Business Profits)

This Article provides rules for the taxation by a Contracting State of the business profits of an enterprise of the other Contracting State. Throughout Article 7, business profits are referred to simply as "profits," consistent with the OECD Model and many other U.S. income tax treaties. The term as used here means profits from a business.

*Paragraph 1*

Paragraph 1 states the general rule that business profits of an enterprise of one Contracting State may not be taxed by the other Contracting State unless the enterprise carries on business in that other Contracting State through a permanent establishment (as defined in Article 5 (Permanent Establishment)) situated there. When that condition is met, the State in which the permanent establishment is situated may tax the enterprise, but only on a net basis and only on the income that is attributable to the permanent establishment. This paragraph is identical to paragraph 1 of Article 7 of the U.S. and OECD Models.

Paragraph 4 of the Protocol incorporates into the Convention the rule of Code section 864(c)(6). Like the Code section on which it is based, paragraph 4 provides that any income or gain attributable to a permanent establishment or a fixed base during its existence is taxable in the Contracting State where the permanent establishment or fixed base is situated, even if the payment of that income or gain is deferred until after the permanent establishment or fixed base ceases to exist. This rule applies with respect to paragraphs 1 and 2 of Article 7 (Business Profits), paragraph 6 of Article 10 (Dividends), paragraph 3 of Articles 11 (Interest), 12 (Royalties) and 13 (Gains), Article 14 (Independent Personal Services) and paragraph 2 of Article 22 (Other Income).

The effect of this rule can be illustrated by the following example. Assume a company that is a resident of the other Contracting State and that maintains a permanent establishment in the United States winds up the permanent establishment's business and sells the permanent establishment's inventory and assets to a U.S. buyer at the end of year 1 in exchange for an interest-bearing installment obligation payable in full at the end of year 3. Despite the fact that Article 13's threshold requirement for U.S. taxation is not met in year 3 because the company has no permanent establishment in the United States, the United States may tax the deferred income payment recognized by the company in year 3.

*Paragraph 2*

Paragraph 2 provides rules for the attribution of business profits to a permanent establishment. The Contracting States will attribute to a permanent establishment the profits that it would have earned had it been an independent enterprise engaged in the same or similar activities under the same or similar circumstances. This language incorporates the arm's-length standard for purposes of determining the profits attributable to a permanent establishment. The computation of business profits attributable to a permanent establishment under this paragraph is subject to the rules of paragraph 3 for the allowance of expenses incurred for the purposes of earning the profits.

The "attributable to" concept of paragraph 2 is analogous but not entirely equivalent to the "effectively connected" concept in Code section 864(c). The profits attributable to a permanent establishment may be from sources within or without a Contracting State. This provision differs from the rule in the prior Convention, which does not include the "attributable to" concept and therefore does not allow the United States to tax non-U.S.-source income of a U.S. permanent establishment of an Irish enterprise.

*Paragraph 3*

Paragraph 3 follows paragraph 3 of Article 7 of the U.S. Model. It is in substance the same as paragraph 3 of Article 7 of the OECD Model, although it is in some respects more detailed. This paragraph provides that, in determining the business profits of a permanent establishment, deductions shall be allowed for the expenses incurred for the purposes of the permanent establishment, ensuring that business profits will be taxed on a net basis. This rule is not limited to expenses incurred exclusively for the purposes of the permanent establishment, but includes a reasonable allocation of expenses incurred for the purposes of the enterprise as a whole, or that part of the enterprise that includes the permanent establishment. Deductions are to be allowed regardless of which accounting unit of the enterprise books the expenses, so long as they are incurred for the purposes of the permanent establishment. For example, a portion of the interest expense recorded on the books of the home office in one State may be deducted by a permanent establishment in the other if properly allocable thereto.

The paragraph specifies that the expenses that may be considered to be incurred for the purposes of the permanent establishment include expenses for research and development, interest and other similar expenses, as well as a reasonable amount of executive and general administrative expenses. This rule permits (but does not require) each Contracting State to apply the type of expense allocation rules provided by U.S. law (such as in Treas. Reg. sections 1.861-8 and 1.882-5).

Paragraph 3 does not permit a deduction for expenses charged to a permanent establishment by another unit of the enterprise. Thus, a permanent establishment may not deduct a royalty deemed paid to the head office. Similarly, a permanent establishment may not increase its business profits by the amount of any notional fees for ancillary services performed for another unit of the enterprise, but also should not receive a deduction for the expense of providing such services, since those expenses would be incurred for purposes of a business unit other than the permanent establishment.

*Paragraph 4*

Paragraph 4 corresponds to paragraph 4 of Article 7 of the OECD Model and provides that a Contracting State in certain circumstances may determine the profits attributable to a permanent establishment on the basis of an apportionment of the total profits of the enterprise. A total profits method may be employed by a Contracting State if it has been customary in that State to use the method even though the figure may differ to some extent from a separate enterprise method so long as the result is in accordance with the principles of Article 7 (i.e., the application of the arm's length standard). Although this paragraph is not included in the U.S. Model, this is not a substantive difference, because the result provided by paragraph 4 is consistent with the rest of Article 7.

The U.S. view is that paragraphs 2 and 3 of Article 7 authorize the use of total profits methods independently of paragraph 4 of Article 7 of the OECD Model because total profits methods are acceptable methods for determining the arm's length profits of affiliated enterprises under Article 9. Accordingly, it is understood that, under paragraph 2 of the Convention, it is permissible to use methods other than separate accounting to estimate the arm's-length profits of a permanent establishment where it is necessary to do so for practical reasons, such as when the affairs of the permanent establishment are so closely bound up with those of the head office that it would be impossible to disentangle them on any strict basis of accounts. Any such approach, like any approach used under paragraph 4, is acceptable only if it approximates the result that would be achieved under an approach based on separate accounting. This view is confirmed by the OECD Commentaries on paragraphs 2 and 3 of Article 7.

*Paragraph 5*

Paragraph 5 provides that no business profits can be attributed to a permanent establishment merely because it purchases goods or merchandise for the enterprise of which it is a part. This paragraph is identical to paragraph 5 of Article 7 of the OECD Model. This rule applies only to an office that performs functions for the enterprise in addition to purchasing. The income attribution issue does not arise if the sole activity of the permanent establishment is the purchase of goods or merchandise because such activity does not give rise to a permanent establishment under Article 5 (Permanent Establishment). A common situation in which paragraph 5 is relevant is one in which a permanent establishment purchases raw materials for the enterprise's manufacturing operation conducted outside the United States and sells the manufactured product. While business profits may be attributable to the permanent establishment with respect to its sales activities, no profits are attributable to it with respect to its purchasing activities.

*Paragraph 6*

Paragraph 6 provides that the business profits attributed to a permanent establishment include only those derived from that permanent establishment's assets or activities. Paragraph 1 of the diplomatic notes further explains that the assets of a permanent establishment include any property or rights used by or held by or for such permanent establishment. This rule is consistent with the "asset-use" and "business activities" test of Code section 864(c)(2). The OECD Model does not expressly provide such a limitation, although it generally is understood to be implicit in paragraph 1 of Article 7 of the OECD Model. This provision makes it clear that the limited force of attraction rule of Code section 864(c)(3) does not apply under the Convention.

This paragraph also tracks paragraph 6 of Article 7 of the OECD Model, providing that profits shall be determined by the same method of accounting each year, unless there is good reason to change the method used. This rule assures consistent tax treatment over time for permanent establishments. It limits the ability of both the Contracting State and the enterprise to change accounting methods to be applied to the permanent establishment. It does not, however, restrict a Contracting State from imposing additional requirements, such as the rules under Code section 481, to prevent amounts from being duplicated or omitted following a change in accounting method.

*Paragraph 7*

The term "profits" is understood generally to mean income derived from any trade or business. In accordance with this broad definition, the term "profits" includes income attributable to notional principal contracts and other financial instruments to the extent that the income is attributable to a trade or business of dealing in such instruments, or is otherwise related to a trade or business (as in the case of a notional principal contract entered into for the purpose of hedging currency risk arising from an active trade or business). Any other income derived from such instruments is, unless specifically covered in another article, dealt with under Article 22 (Other Income).

The paragraph states the longstanding U.S. view that income earned by an enterprise from the furnishing of personal services is business profits. Thus, a consulting firm resident in one

State whose employees perform services in the other State through a permanent establishment may be taxed in that other State on a net basis under Article 7, and not under Article 14 (Independent Personal Services), which applies only to individuals. The salaries of the employees would be subject to the rules of Article 15 (Dependent Personal Services).

The paragraph also specifies that the term "profits" includes income derived by an enterprise from the rental of tangible movable property. The use of the term "tangible movable property" follows the OECD Model and reflects no substantive difference from the term "tangible personal property" used in the U.S. Model. The inclusion of income derived by an enterprise from the rental of tangible movable property in business profits means that such income earned by a resident of a Contracting State can be taxed by the other Contracting State only if the income is attributable to a permanent establishment maintained by the resident in that other State, and, if the income is taxable, it can be taxed only on a net basis. Income from the rental of tangible movable property that is not derived in connection with a trade or business is dealt with in Article 22 (Other Income).

*Paragraph 8*

Paragraph 8 coordinates the provisions of Article 7 and other provisions of the Convention. Under this paragraph, when business profits include items of income that are dealt with separately under other articles of the Convention, the provisions of those articles will, except when they specifically provide to the contrary, take precedence over the provisions of Article 7. For example, the taxation of dividends will be determined by the rules of Article 10 (Dividends), and not by Article 7, except where, as provided in paragraph 6 of Article 10, the dividend is attributable to a permanent establishment or fixed base. In the latter case the provisions of Articles 7 or 14 (Independent Personal Services) apply. Thus, an enterprise of one State deriving dividends from the other State may not rely on Article 7 to exempt those dividends from tax at source if they are not attributable to a permanent establishment of the enterprise in the other State. By the same token, if the dividends are attributable to a permanent establishment in the other State, the dividends may be taxed on a net income basis at the source State's full corporate tax rate, rather than on a gross basis under Article 10 (Dividends).

As provided in Article 8 (Shipping and Air Transport), income derived from shipping and air transport activities in international traffic described in that Article is taxable only in the country of residence of the enterprise regardless of whether it is attributable to a permanent establishment situated in the source State.

*Relation to Other Articles*

This Article is subject to the saving clause of paragraph 4 of Article 1 (General Scope) of the Model. Thus, if a citizen of the United States who is a resident of Ireland under the treaty derives business profits from the United States that are not attributable to a permanent establishment in the United States, the United States may, subject to the special foreign tax credit rules of paragraph 3 of Article 24 (Relief from Double Taxation), tax those profits, notwithstanding the provision of paragraph 1 of this Article which would exempt the income from U.S. tax.

The benefits of this Article are also subject to Article 23 (Limitation on Benefits). Thus, an enterprise of Ireland that derives income effectively connected with a U.S. trade or business may not claim the benefits of Article 7 unless the resident carrying on the enterprise qualifies for such benefits under Article 23.

## Article 8 (Shipping and Air Transport)

This Article governs the taxation of profits from the operation of ships and aircraft in international traffic. The term "international traffic" is defined in subparagraph 1(d) of Article 3 (General Definitions).

*Paragraph 1*

Paragraph 1 provides that profits derived by an enterprise of a Contracting State from the operation in international traffic of ships or aircraft are taxable only in that Contracting State. Because paragraph 8 of Article 7 (Business Profits) defers to Article 8 with respect to shipping income, such income derived by a resident of one of the Contracting States may not be taxed in the other State even if the enterprise has a permanent establishment in that other State. Thus, if a U.S. airline has a ticket office in Ireland, Ireland may not tax the airline's profits attributable to that office under Article 7. Since entities engaged in international transportation activities normally will have many permanent establishments in a number of countries, the rule avoids difficulties that would be encountered in attributing income to multiple permanent establishments if the income were covered by Article 7 (Business Profits).

*Paragraph 2*

The income from the operation of ships or aircraft in international traffic that is exempt from tax under paragraph 1 is defined in paragraph 2. This paragraph is not found in the OECD Model, but the effect of the paragraph is generally consistent with the description of the scope of Article 8 in the Commentary to Article 8 of the OECD Model. Most of the income items that are described in paragraph 2 are described in the OECD Commentary as being included within the scope of the exemption in paragraph 1. Unlike the OECD Model, however, paragraph 2 also covers non-incidental bareboat leasing. See, paragraph 5 of the OECD Commentaries.

In addition to income derived directly from the operation of ships and aircraft in international traffic, this definition also includes certain items of rental income that are closely related to those activities. First, income of an enterprise of a Contracting State from the rental of ships or aircraft on a full basis (i.e., with crew) when such ships or aircraft are used in international traffic is income of the lessor from the operation of ships and aircraft in international traffic and, therefore, is exempt from tax in the other Contracting State under paragraph 1. Also, paragraph 2 encompasses income from the lease of ships or aircraft on a bareboat basis (i.e., without crew), either when the ships or aircraft are operated in international traffic by the lessee, or when the income is incidental to other income of the lessor from the operation of ships or aircraft in international traffic. As discussed above, of these classes of rental income, only non-incidental, bareboat lease income is not covered by Article 8 of the OECD Model.

Paragraph 2 also clarifies, consistent with the Commentary to Article 8 of the OECD Model, that income earned by an enterprise from the inland transport of property or passengers within either Contracting State falls within Article 8 if the transport is undertaken as part of the international transport of property or passengers by the enterprise. Thus, if a U.S. shipping company contracts to carry property from Ireland to a U.S. city and, as part of that contract, it transports the property by truck from its point of origin to an airport in Ireland (or it contracts with a trucking company to carry the property to the airport), the income earned by the U.S. shipping company from the overland leg of the journey would be taxable only in the United States. Similarly, Article 8 also would apply to income from lighterage undertaken as part of the international transport of goods.

Finally, certain non-transport activities that are an integral part of the services performed by a transport company are understood to be covered in paragraph 1, though they are not specified in paragraph 2. These include, for example, the performance of some maintenance or catering services by one airline for another airline, if these services are incidental to the provision of those services by the airline for itself. Income earned by concessionaires, however, is not covered by Article 8. These interpretations of paragraph 1 also are consistent with the Commentary to Article 8 of the OECD Model.

*Paragraph 3*

Under this paragraph, profits of an enterprise of a Contracting State from the use, maintenance or rental of containers (including equipment for their transport) that are used for the transport of goods in international traffic are exempt from tax in the other Contracting State. This result obtains under paragraph 3 regardless of whether the recipient of the income is engaged in the operation of ships or aircraft in international traffic, and regardless of whether the enterprise has a permanent establishment in the other Contracting State. Only income from the use, maintenance or rental of containers that is incidental to other income from international traffic is covered by Article 8 of the OECD Model.

*Paragraph 4*

This paragraph clarifies that the provisions of paragraphs 1 and 3 also apply to profits derived by an enterprise of a Contracting State from participation in a pool, joint business or international operating agency. This refers to various arrangements for international cooperation by carriers in shipping and air transport. For example, airlines from two countries may agree to share the transport of passengers between the two countries. They each will fly the same number of flights per week and share the revenues from that route equally, regardless of the number of passengers that each airline actually transports. Paragraph 4 makes clear that with respect to each carrier the income dealt with in the Article is that carrier's share of the total transport, not the income derived from the passengers actually carried by the airline. This paragraph corresponds to paragraph 4 of Article 8 of the OECD Model.

*Relation to Other Articles*

The taxation of gains from the alienation of ships, aircraft or containers is not dealt with in this Article but in paragraph 4 of Article 13 (Capital Gains).

As with other benefits of the Convention, the benefit of exclusive residence country taxation under Article 8 is available to an enterprise only if it is entitled to benefits under Article 23 (Limitation on Benefits).

This Article also is subject to the saving clause of paragraph 4 of Article 1 (General Scope) of the Model. Thus, if a citizen of the United States who is a resident of Ireland derives profits from the operation of ships or aircraft in international traffic, notwithstanding the exclusive residence country taxation in paragraph 1 of Article 8, the United States may, subject to the special foreign tax credit rules of paragraph 3 of Article 24 (Relief from Double Taxation), tax those profits as part of the worldwide income of the citizen. (This is an unlikely situation, however, because non-tax considerations (e.g., insurance) generally result in shipping activities being carried on in corporate form.)

## Article 9 (Associated Enterprises)

This Article incorporates in the Convention the arm's-length principle reflected in the U.S. domestic transfer pricing provisions, particularly Code section 482. It provides that when related enterprises engage in a transaction on terms that are not arm's-length, the Contracting States may make appropriate adjustments to the taxable income and tax liability of such related enterprises to reflect what the income and tax of these enterprises with respect to the transaction would have been had there been an arm's-length relationship between them.

*Paragraph 1*

This paragraph is essentially the same as its counterpart in the OECD Model. It addresses the situation where an enterprise of a Contracting State is related to an enterprise of the other Contracting State, and there are arrangements or conditions imposed between the enterprises in their commercial or financial relations that are different from those that would have existed in the absence of the relationship. Under these circumstances, the Contracting States may adjust the income (or loss) of the enterprise to reflect what it would have been in the absence of such a relationship.

The paragraph identifies the relationships between enterprises that serve as a prerequisite to application of the Article. As the Commentary to the OECD Model makes clear, the necessary element in these relationships is effective control, which is also the standard for purposes of section 482. Thus, the Article applies if an enterprise of one State participates directly or indirectly in the management, control, or capital of the enterprise of the other State. Also, the Article applies if any third person or persons participate directly or indirectly in the management, control, or capital of enterprises of different States. For this purpose, all types of control are included, i.e., whether or not legally enforceable and however exercised or exercisable.

The fact that a transaction is entered into between such related enterprises does not, in and of itself, mean that a Contracting State may adjust the income (or loss) of one or both of the enterprises under the provisions of this Article. If the conditions of the transaction are consistent with those that would be made between independent persons, the income arising from that transaction should not be subject to adjustment under this Article.

Similarly, the fact that associated enterprises may have concluded arrangements, such as cost sharing arrangements or general services agreements, is not in itself an indication that the two enterprises have entered into a non-arm's-length transaction that should give rise to an adjustment under paragraph 1. Both related and unrelated parties enter into such arrangements (e.g., joint venturers may share some development costs). As with any other kind of transaction, when related parties enter into an arrangement, the specific arrangement must be examined to see whether or not it meets the arm's-length standard. In the event that it does not, an appropriate adjustment may be made, which may include modifying the terms of the agreement or re-characterizing the transaction to reflect its substance.

It is understood that the "commensurate with income" standard for determining appropriate transfer prices for intangibles, added to Code section 482 by the Tax Reform Act of 1986, was designed to operate consistently with the arm's-length standard. The implementation of this standard in the section 482 regulations is in accordance with the general principles of paragraph 1 of Article 9 of the Convention, as interpreted by the OECD Transfer Pricing Guidelines.

It is understood that nothing in paragraph 1 limits the rights of the Contracting States to apply their internal law provisions relating to adjustments between related parties. They also reserve the right to make adjustments in cases involving tax evasion or fraud. Such adjustments -- the distribution, apportionment, or allocation of income, deductions, credits or allowances -- are permitted even if they are different from, or go beyond, those authorized by paragraph 1 of the Article, as long as they accord with the general principles of paragraph 1, i.e., that the adjustment reflects what would have transpired had the related parties been acting at arm's length. For example, while paragraph 1 explicitly allows adjustments of deductions in computing taxable income, it does not deal with adjustments to tax credits. It does not, however, preclude such adjustments if they can be made under internal law. The OECD Model reaches the same result. See paragraph 4 of the Commentaries to Article 9.

This Article also permits tax authorities to deal with thin capitalization issues. They may, in the context of Article 9, scrutinize more than the rate of interest charged on a loan between related persons. They also may examine the capital structure of an enterprise, whether a payment in respect of that loan should be treated as interest, and, if it is treated as interest, under what circumstances interest deductions should be allowed to the payor. Paragraph 2 of the Commentaries to Article 9 of the OECD Model, together with the U.S. observation set forth in paragraph 15, sets forth a similar understanding of the scope of Article 9 in the context of thin capitalization.

*Paragraph 2*

When a Contracting State has made an adjustment that is consistent with the provisions of paragraph 1, and the other Contracting State agrees that the adjustment was appropriate to reflect arm's-length conditions, that other Contracting State is obligated to make a correlative adjustment (sometimes referred to as a "corresponding adjustment") to the tax liability of the related person in that other Contracting State. Although the OECD Model does not specify that the other Contracting State must agree with the initial adjustment before it is obligated to make the correlative adjustment, the Commentary makes clear that the paragraph is to be read that way.

As explained in the OECD Commentaries, Article 9 leaves the treatment of "secondary adjustments" to the laws of the Contracting States. When an adjustment under Article 9 has been made, one of the parties will have in its possession funds that it would not have had at arm's length. The question arises as to how to treat these funds. In the United States the general practice is to treat such funds as a dividend or contribution to capital, depending on the relationship between the parties. Under certain circumstances, the parties may be permitted to restore the funds to the party that would have the funds at arm's length, and to establish an account payable pending restoration of the funds. See, Rev. Proc. 65-17, 1965-1 C.B. 833.

The Contracting State making a secondary adjustment will take the other provisions of the Convention, where relevant, into account. For example, if the effect of a secondary adjustment is to treat a U.S. corporation as having made a distribution of profits to its parent corporation in Ireland, the provisions of Article 10 (Dividends) will apply, and the United States may impose a 5 percent withholding tax on the dividend. Also, if under Article 24, Ireland generally gives a credit for taxes paid with respect to such dividends, it would also be required to do so in this case.

The competent authorities are authorized by paragraph 2 to consult, if necessary, to resolve any differences in the application of these provisions. For example, there may be a disagreement over whether an adjustment made by a Contracting State under paragraph 1 was appropriate.

If a correlative adjustment is made under paragraph 2, it is to be implemented, pursuant to paragraph 2 of Article 26 (Mutual Agreement Procedure), notwithstanding any time limits or other procedural limitations in the law of the Contracting State making the adjustment. If a taxpayer has entered a closing agreement (or other written settlement) with the United States prior to bringing a case to the competent authorities, the U.S. competent authority will endeavor only to obtain a correlative adjustment from Ireland. See, Rev. Proc. 96-13, 1996-13 I.R.B. 31, Section 7.05.

*Relationship to Other Articles*

The saving clause of paragraph 4 of Article 1 (General Scope) does not apply to paragraph 2 of Article 9 by virtue of the exceptions to the saving clause in paragraph 5(a) of Article 1. Thus, even if the statute of limitations has run, a refund of tax can be made in order to implement a correlative adjustment. Statutory or procedural limitations, however, cannot be overridden to impose additional tax, because paragraph 2 of Article 1 provides that the Convention cannot restrict any statutory benefit.

### Article 10 (Dividends)

Article 10 provides rules for the taxation of dividends paid by a resident of one Contracting State to a beneficial owner that is a resident of the other Contracting State. The article provides for full residence country taxation of such dividends and a limited source-State right to tax. The Article contains two alternatives for the taxation of dividends, depending on whether Ireland continues to allow a tax credit to individual shareholders in respect of dividends from a corporation which is a resident of Ireland. Article 10 also provides rules for the imposition of a tax on branch profits by the State of source.

*Paragraph 1*

The right of a shareholder's country of residence to tax dividends arising in the source country is preserved by paragraph 1, which permits a Contracting State to tax its residents on dividends paid to them by a resident of the other Contracting State. For dividends from any other source paid to a resident, Article 22 (Other Income) grants the residence country exclusive taxing jurisdiction (other than for dividends attributable to a permanent establishment or fixed base in the other State).

*Paragraph 2*

The State of source may also tax dividends beneficially owned by a resident of the other State, subject to the limitations in paragraph 2. Generally, the source State's tax is limited to 15 percent of the gross amount of the dividend paid. If, however, the beneficial owner of the dividends is a company resident in the other State that holds at least 10 percent of the voting shares of the company paying the dividend, then the source State's tax is limited to 5 percent of the gross amount of the dividend. Indirect ownership of voting shares (through tiers of corporations) and direct ownership of non-voting shares are not taken into account for purposes of determining eligibility for the 5 percent direct dividend rate. Shares are considered voting shares if they provide the power to elect, appoint or replace any person vested with the powers ordinarily exercised by the board of directors of a U.S. corporation.

The benefits of paragraph 2 may be granted at the time of payment by means of reduced withholding at source. It also is consistent with the paragraph for tax to be withheld at the time of payment at full statutory rates, and the treaty benefit to be granted by means of a subsequent refund.

Paragraph 2 does not affect the taxation of the profits out of which the dividends are paid. The taxation by a Contracting State of the income of its resident companies is governed by the internal law of the Contracting State, subject to the provisions of paragraph 4 of Article 25 (Non-Discrimination).

The term "beneficial owner" is not defined in the Convention, and is, therefore, defined as under the internal law of the country imposing tax (i.e., the source country). The beneficial owner of the dividend for purposes of Article 10 is the person to which the dividend income is attributable for tax purposes under the laws of the source State. Thus, if a dividend paid by a corporation that is a resident of one of the States (as determined under Article 4 (Residence)) is received by a nominee or agent that is a resident of the other State on behalf of a person that is not a resident of that other State, the dividend is not entitled to the benefits of this Article. However, a dividend received by a nominee on behalf of a resident of that other State would be entitled to benefits. These limitations are confirmed by paragraph 12 of the OECD Commentaries to Article 10. See also, paragraph 24 of the OECD Commentaries to Article 1 (General Scope).

Companies holding shares through fiscally transparent entities such as partnerships are considered for purposes of this paragraph to hold their proportionate interest in the shares held by the intermediate entity. As a result, companies holding shares through such entities may be able to claim the benefits of subparagraph (a) under certain circumstances. The lower rate applies when the company's proportionate share of the shares held by the intermediate entity meets the 10 percent voting stock threshold. Whether this ownership threshold is satisfied may be difficult to determine and often will require an analysis of the partnership or trust agreement.

*Paragraph 3*

Paragraph 3 applies where, as at the present time, an individual resident in Ireland is entitled to a credit in respect of dividends paid by a corporation that is a resident of Ireland. So long as this system remains in force, only paragraph 3, and not paragraph 2, shall apply to such dividends.

The tax credit referred to in Paragraph 3 is allowed pursuant to Ireland's system of integrating corporate and shareholder taxation. Under the system adopted by Ireland, "advance corporation tax" ("ACT") is collected at the corporate level upon a distribution of dividends by the corporation. This tax is treated both as an advance payment of a portion of the corporate income tax, and also as a payment by an individual Irish resident shareholder in partial or complete satisfaction of his personal tax liabilities on the dividend. Paragraph 3 provides a mechanism by which United States shareholders of an Irish corporation will receive the benefits of the shareholder credits which have heretofore not been granted to United States residents.

In the case of United States shareholders other than corporations which control at least 10 percent of the voting stock of the Irish resident corporation, the Irish refund will equal the full credit payable to an individual resident in Ireland, less 15 percent of the aggregate amount of the dividend and the Irish credit. For United States tax purposes, the Irish credit shall be treated as additional gross income and the 15 percent withholding tax will be considered a tax on the shareholder. At current rates of tax, the result is as follows:

| | |
|---|---|
| Dividend | $ 79.00 |
| Irish credit | 21.00 |
| Gross dividend | 100.00 |
| | |
| Irish withholding tax | 15.00 |
| U.S. foreign tax credit | 15.00 |

With respect to dividends paid by a corporation resident in Ireland to a United States corporation which either alone or together with one or more associated corporations controls, directly or indirectly, at least 10 percent of the voting stock of the Irish resident that is paying the dividend, the shareholder will not be entitled to a tax credit, but the dividend will be exempt from Irish taxation at the shareholder level. For these purposes, two companies shall be deemed to be associated if one is controlled directly or indirectly by the other or both are controlled directly or indirectly by a third company.

*Paragraph 4*

Paragraph 4 provides rules that modify the maximum rates of tax at source provided in paragraph 2 in particular cases. The first sentence of paragraph 4 denies the lower direct investment withholding rate of paragraph 2(a) for dividends paid by a U.S. Regulated Investment Company (RIC) or a U.S. Real Estate Investment Trust (REIT). The second sentence denies the benefits of both subparagraphs (a) and (b) of paragraph 2 to dividends paid by REITs in certain circumstances, allowing them to be taxed at the U.S. statutory rate (30 percent). The United States limits the source tax on dividends paid by a REIT to the 15 percent rate when the beneficial owner of the dividend is an individual resident of the other State that owns a less than 10 percent interest in the REIT. These exceptions to the general rules of paragraph 2 have been part of U.S. tax treaty policy since 1988.

The denial of the 5 percent withholding rate at source to all RIC and REIT shareholders, and the denial of the 15 percent rate to all but small individual shareholders of REITs is intended to prevent the use of these entities to gain unjustifiable source taxation benefits for certain shareholders resident in the other Contracting State. For example, a corporation resident in Ireland that wishes to hold a diversified portfolio of U.S. corporate shares may hold the portfolio directly and pay a U.S. withholding tax of 15 percent on all of the dividends that it receives. Alternatively, it may acquire a diversified portfolio by purchasing shares in a RIC. Since the RIC may be a pure conduit, there may be no U.S. tax costs to interposing the RIC in the chain of ownership. Absent the special rule in paragraph 2, use of the RIC could transform portfolio dividends, taxable in the United States under the Convention at 15 percent, into direct investment dividends taxable at only 5 percent.

Similarly, a resident of Ireland directly holding U.S. real property would pay U.S. tax either at a 30 percent rate on the gross income or at graduated rates on the net income (up to 39.6 percent in the case of individuals and up to 35 percent in the case of corporations). As in the preceding example, by placing the real property in a REIT, the investor could transform real estate income into dividend income, taxable at the rates provided in Article 10, significantly reducing the U.S. tax burden that otherwise would be imposed. To prevent this circumvention of U.S. rules applicable to real property, most REIT shareholders are subject to 30 percent tax at source. However, since a relatively small individual investor might be subject to a U.S. tax of 15 percent of the net income even if he earned the real estate income directly, individuals who hold less than a 10 percent interest in the REIT remain taxable at source at a 15 percent rate.

*Paragraph 5*

Paragraph 5 defines the term dividends broadly and flexibly. The definition is intended to cover all arrangements that yield a return on an equity investment in a corporation as determined under the tax law of the state of source, as well as arrangements that might be developed in the future.

The term dividends includes income from shares, or other rights that are not treated as debt under the law of the source State. The term also includes income that is subjected to the same tax treatment as income from shares by the law of the State of source. Thus, a constructive dividend that results from a non-arm's length transaction between a corporation and a related party is a dividend. In the case of the United States the term dividend includes amounts treated as a dividend under U.S. law upon the sale or redemption of shares or upon a transfer of shares in a reorganization. See, e.g., Rev. Rul. 92-85, 1992-2 C.B. 69 (sale of foreign subsidiary's stock to U.S. sister company is a deemed dividend to extent of subsidiary's and sister's earnings and profits). Further, a distribution from a U.S. publicly traded limited partnership, which is taxed as a corporation under U.S. law, is a dividend for purposes of Article 10. However, a distribution by a limited liability company is not taxable by the United States under Article 10, provided the limited liability company is not characterized as an association taxable as a corporation under U.S. law.

Under U.S. law, a payment denominated as interest that is made by a thinly capitalized corporation may be treated as a dividend to the extent that the debt is recharacterized as equity under the laws of the source State. Paragraph 5 of the Protocol provides that the term "dividends" does not include interest that is recharacterized as dividends because it is paid to a non-resident company, except to the extent that it exceeds an arm's length amount. This rule is not intended to limit the ability of the United States to apply its thin capitalization rules, which apply without regard to the identity of the beneficial owner of the income. Rather, it is to deal with the situation where all interest paid to non-resident companies is treated as dividends without regard to whether the payor is thinly capitalized or the amount of the payment is other than an arm's length amount.

*Paragraph 6*

Paragraph 6 excludes from the general source country limitations under paragraph 2 dividends paid with respect to holdings that form part of the business property of a permanent establishment or a fixed base. Such dividends will be taxed on a net basis using the rates and rules of taxation generally applicable to residents of the State in which the permanent establishment or fixed base is located, as modified by the Convention. An example of dividends paid with respect to the business property of a permanent establishment would be dividends derived by a dealer in stock or securities from stock or securities that the dealer held for sale to customers.

*Paragraph 7*

Paragraph 7 permits a State to impose a branch profits tax on a company resident in the other State. The tax is in addition to other taxes permitted by the Convention.

A State may impose a branch profits tax on a company if the company has income attributable to a permanent establishment in that State, derives income from real property in that State that is taxed on a net basis under Article 6, or realizes gains taxable in that State under paragraph 1 of Article 13. The tax is limited, however, to the aforementioned items of income that are included in the "dividend equivalent amount" in the case of the United States, and the amount that would be distributed as a dividend if earned by a subsidiary rather than a branch, in the case of Ireland.

Paragraph 7 permits the United States generally to impose its branch profits tax on a corporation resident in Ireland to the extent of the corporation's (i) business profits that are attributable to a permanent establishment in the United States (ii) income that is subject to taxation on a net basis because the corporation has elected under section 882(d) of the Code to treat income from real property not otherwise taxed on a net basis as effectively connected income and (iii) gain from the disposition of a United States Real Property Interest, other than an interest in a United States Real Property Holding Corporation. The United States may not impose its branch profits tax on the business profits of a corporation resident in the other State that are effectively connected with a U.S. trade or business but that are not attributable to a permanent establishment and are not otherwise subject to U.S. taxation under Article 6 or paragraph 1 of Article 13.

The term "dividend equivalent amount" used in paragraph 7 has the same meaning that it has under section 884 of the Code, as amended from time to time, provided the amendments are consistent with the purpose of the branch profits tax. Generally, the dividend equivalent amount for a particular year is the income described above that is included in the corporation's effectively connected earnings and profits for that year, after payment of the corporate tax under Articles 6, 7 or 13, reduced for any increase in the branch's U.S. net equity during the year and increased for any reduction in its U.S. net equity during the year. U.S. net equity is U.S. assets less U.S. liabilities. See, Treas. Reg. section 1.884-1. The dividend equivalent amount for any year approximates the dividend that a U.S. branch office would have paid during the year if the branch had been operated as a separate U.S. subsidiary company. This is analogous to the amount that Ireland may tax under subparagraph (b).

*Paragraph 8*

Paragraph 8 provides that the branch profits tax permitted by paragraph 7 shall not be imposed at a rate exceeding the direct investment dividend withholding rate of five percent.

*Relation to Other Articles*

Notwithstanding the foregoing limitations on source country taxation of dividends, the saving clause of paragraph 3 of Article 1 permits the United States to tax dividends received by its residents and citizens, subject to the special foreign tax credit rules of paragraph 3 of Article 24 (Relief from Double Taxation), as if the Convention had not come into effect.

The benefits of this Article are also subject to the provisions of Article 23 (Limitation on Benefits). Thus, if a resident of Ireland is the beneficial owner of dividends paid by a U.S. corporation, the shareholder must qualify for treaty benefits under at least one of the tests of Article 23 in order to receive the benefits of this Article.


## Article 11 (Interest)

Article 11 specifies the taxing jurisdictions over interest income of the States of source and residence and defines the terms necessary to apply the article.

*Paragraph 1*

This paragraph grants to the State of residence the exclusive right, subject to exceptions provided in paragraph 3 of Article 11 and paragraph 6 of the Protocol, to tax interest beneficially owned by its residents and arising in the other Contracting State.

The term "beneficial owner" is not defined in the Convention, and is, therefore, defined as under the internal law of the country imposing tax (i.e., the source country). The beneficial owner of interest for purposes of Article 11 is the person to which the interest income is attributable for tax purposes under the laws of the source State. Thus, if interest arising in one of the States is received by a nominee or agent that is a resident of the other State on behalf of a person that is not a resident of that other State, the interest is not entitled to the benefits of this Article. However, interest received by a nominee on behalf of a resident of that other State would be entitled to benefits. These limitations are confirmed by paragraph 8 of the OECD Commentaries to Article 11. See also, paragraph 24 of the OECD Commentaries to Article 1 (General Scope).

Paragraph 6 of the Protocol provides anti-abuse exceptions to the source-country exemption in paragraph 1 for two classes of interest payments.

The first exception deals with so-called "contingent interest." Under this provision interest arising in the United States that is determined by reference to the profits of the issuer or to the profits of one of its associated enterprises, and paid to a resident of the other State may be taxed by the United States according to its domestic laws, but if the beneficial owner is a resident of the other Contracting State, the gross amount of the interest may be taxed at a rate not exceeding the rate prescribed in subparagraph b) of paragraph 2 of Article 10 (Dividends).

The second exception is consistent with the policy of Code sections 860E(e) and 860G(b) that excess inclusions with respect to a real estate mortgage investment conduit (REMIC) should bear full U.S. tax in all cases. Without a full tax at source foreign purchasers of residual interests would have a competitive advantage over U.S. purchasers at the time these interests are initially offered. Also, absent this rule the U.S. fisc would suffer a revenue loss with respect to mortgages held in a REMIC because of opportunities for tax avoidance created by differences in the timing of taxable and economic income produced by these interests.

*Paragraph 2*

The term "interest" as used in Article 11 is defined in paragraph 2 to include, inter alia, income from debt claims of every kind, whether or not secured by a mortgage. Penalty charges for late payment of taxes are excluded from the definition of interest. Interest that is paid or accrued subject to a contingency is within the ambit of Article 11. This includes income from a debt obligation carrying the right to participate in profits. The term does not, however, include amounts that are treated as dividends under Article 10 (Dividends).

The term interest also includes amounts subject to the same tax treatment as income from money lent under the law of the State in which the income arises. Thus, for purposes of the Article, amounts that the United States will treat as interest include (i) the difference between the issue price and the stated redemption price at maturity of a debt instrument, i.e., original issue discount (OID), which may be wholly or partially realized on the disposition of a debt instrument (section 1273), (ii) amounts that are imputed interest on a deferred sales contract (section 483),

(iii) amounts treated as OID under the stripped bond rules (section 1286), (iv) amounts treated as original issue discount under the below-market interest rate rules (section 7872), (v) a partner's distributive share of a partnership's interest income (section 702), (vi) the interest portion of periodic payments made under a "finance lease" or similar contractual arrangement that in substance is a borrowing by the nominal lessee to finance the acquisition of property, (vii) amounts included in the income of a holder of a residual interest in a REMIC (section 860E), because these amounts generally are subject to the same taxation treatment as interest under U.S. tax law, and (viii) embedded interest with respect to notional principal contracts.

*Paragraph 3*

Paragraph 3 provides an exception to the exclusive residence taxation rule of paragraph 1 in cases where the beneficial owner of the interest carries on business through a permanent establishment in the State of source or performs independent personal services from a fixed base situated in that State and the interest is attributable to that permanent establishment or fixed base. In such cases the provisions of Article 7 (Business Profits) or Article 14 (Independent Personal Services) will apply and the State of source will retain the right to impose tax on such interest income.

In the case of a permanent establishment or fixed base that once existed in the State but that no longer exists, the provisions of paragraph 3 also apply, by virtue of paragraph 4 of the Protocol, to interest that would be attributable to such a permanent establishment or fixed base if it did exist in the year of payment or accrual. See the Technical Explanation of paragraph 1 of Article 7.

*Paragraph 4*

Paragraph 4 provides a source rule for interest. Under this paragraph, interest is deemed to arise in a Contracting State when the payor is a resident of that State, or the payor, whether a resident of a Contracting State or not, has in that Contracting State a permanent establishment or fixed base in connection with which the indebtedness on which the interest paid was incurred and such interest is borne by such permanent establishment or fixed base. This source rule corresponds to paragraph 5 of Article 11 of the OECD Model.

*Paragraph 5*

Paragraph 5 provides that in cases involving special relationships between persons, Article 11 applies only to that portion of the total interest payments that would have been made absent such special relationships (i.e., an arm's-length interest payment). Any excess amount of interest paid remains taxable according to the laws of the United States and the other Contracting State, respectively, with due regard to the other provisions of the Convention. Thus, if the excess amount would be treated under the source country's law as a distribution of profits by a corporation, such amount could be taxed as a dividend rather than as interest, but the tax would be subject, if appropriate, to the rate limitations of paragraph 2 of Article 10 (Dividends).

The term "special relationship" is not defined in the Convention. In applying this paragraph the United States considers the term to include the relationships described in Article 9, which in turn corresponds to the definition of "control" for purposes of section 482 of the Code.

This paragraph does not address cases where, owing to a special relationship between the payer and the beneficial owner or between both of them and some other person, the amount of the interest is less than an arm's-length amount. In those cases a transaction may be characterized to reflect its substance and interest may be imputed consistent with the definition of interest in paragraph 2. The United States would apply section 482 or 7872 of the Code to determine the amount of imputed interest in those cases.

*Paragraph 6*

Paragraph 6 provides that the excess of the amount deductible by a permanent establishment in the United States of a company which is a resident of Ireland over the interest actually paid by such permanent establishment, as those amounts are determined pursuant to the laws of the United States, shall be treated as interest beneficially owned by a resident of Ireland. Thus, the Article 11 exemption from source country taxation will generally prevent the United States from collecting the excess interest tax imposed by section 884(f) of the Code on a resident of Ireland. This provision generally is not included in U.S. tax treaties because it is the result provided by U.S. law when interest is exempt from tax at source and therefore does not need to be stated in the treaty.

*Relation to Other Articles*

Notwithstanding the foregoing limitations on source country taxation of interest, the saving clause of paragraph 4 of Article 1 permits the United States to tax its residents and citizens, subject to the special foreign tax credit rules of paragraph 3 of Article 24 (Relief from Double Taxation), as if the Convention had not come into force.

As with other benefits of the Convention, the benefits of exclusive residence State taxation of interest under paragraph 1 of Article 11, or limited source taxation under paragraph 6 of the Protocol, are available to a resident of the other State only if that resident is entitled to those benefits under the provisions of Article 23 (Limitation on Benefits).


### Article 12 (Royalties)

Article 12 specifies the taxing jurisdiction over royalties of the States of residence and source and defines the terms necessary to apply the article.

*Paragraph 1*

Paragraph 1 grants to the state of residence of the beneficial owner of royalties the exclusive right to tax royalties arising in the other Contracting State, subject to exceptions provided in paragraph 3 (for royalties taxable as business profits and independent personal services).

The term "beneficial owner" is not defined in the Convention, and is, therefore, defined as under the internal law of the country imposing tax (i.e., the source country). The beneficial owner of royalties for purposes of Article 12 is the person to which the royalty income is attributable for tax purposes under the laws of the source State. Thus, if royalties arising in one of the States is received by a nominee or agent that is a resident of the other State on behalf of a person that is not a resident of that other State, the royalties are not entitled to the benefits of this Article. However, royalties received by a nominee on behalf of a resident of that other State would be entitled to benefits. These limitations are confirmed by paragraph 4 of the OECD Commentaries to Article 12. See also, paragraph 24 of the OECD Commentaries to Article 1 (General Scope).

*Paragraph 2*

The term "royalties" as used in Article 12 is defined in paragraph 2 to include payments of any kind received as a consideration for the use of, or the right to use, any copyright of a literary, artistic, scientific or other work; for the use of, or the right to use, any patent, trademark, design or model, plan, secret formula or process, or other like right or property; or for information concerning industrial, commercial, or scientific experience. It does not include income from leasing personal property. Like the U.S., but unlike the OECD, Model, paragraph 1 does not refer to an amount "paid" to a resident of the other Contracting State. The deletion of this term is intended to eliminate any inference that an amount must actually be paid to the resident before it is subject to the provisions of Article 12. Under paragraph 1, an amount that is accrued but not paid also would fall within Article 12.

The term royalties is defined in the Convention and therefore is generally independent of domestic law. Certain terms used in the definition are not defined in the Convention, but these may be defined under domestic tax law. For example, the term "secret process or formulas" is found in the Code, and its meaning has been elaborated in the context of sections 351 and 367. See Rev. Rul. 55-17, 1955-1 C.B. 388; Rev. Rul. 64-56, 1964-1 C.B. 133; Rev. Proc. 69-19, 1969-2 C.B. 301.

Consideration for the use or right to use cinematographic films, or works on film, tape, or disks in radio or television broadcasting is specifically included in the definition of royalties. It is intended that subsequent technological advances in the field of radio and television broadcasting will not affect the inclusion of payments relating to the use of such means of reproduction in the definition of royalties.

If an artist who is resident in one Contracting State records a performance in the other Contracting State, retains a copyrighted interest in a recording, and receives payments for the right to use the recording based on the sale or public playing of the recording, then the right of such other Contracting State to tax those payments is governed by Article 12. See Boulez v. Commissioner, 83 T.C. 584 (1984), aff'd, 810 F.2d 209 (D.C. Cir. 1986).

Computer software generally is protected by copyright laws around the world. While not explicitly stated, it is mutually understood that, under the Convention, consideration received for the use or the right to use computer software is treated either as royalties or as business profits, depending on the facts and circumstances of the transaction giving rise to the payment. It is also understood that payments received in connection with the transfer of so-called "shrink-wrap" computer software are treated as business profits.

The term "royalties" also includes gain derived from the alienation of any right or property that would give rise to royalties, to the extent the gain is contingent on the productivity, use, or further alienation thereof. Gains that are not so contingent are dealt with under Article 13 (Capital Gains).

The term "industrial, commercial, or scientific experience" (sometimes referred to as "know-how") has the meaning ascribed to it in paragraph 11 of the Commentary to Article 12 of the OECD Model Convention. Consistent with that meaning, the term may include information that is ancillary to a right otherwise giving rise to royalties, such as a patent or secret process.

Know-how also may include, in limited cases, technical information that is conveyed through technical or consultancy services. It does not include general educational training of the user's employees, nor does it include information developed especially for the user, for example, a technical plan or design developed according to the user's specifications. Thus, as provided in paragraph 11 of the Commentaries to Article 12 of the OECD Model, the term "royalties" does not include payments received as consideration for after-sales service, for services rendered by a seller to a purchaser under a guarantee, or for pure technical assistance.

The term "royalties" also does not include payments for professional services (such as architectural, engineering, legal, managerial, medical, or software development services). For example, income from the design of a refinery by an engineer (even if the engineer employed know-how in the process of rendering the design) or the production of a legal brief by a lawyer is not income from the transfer of know-how taxable under Article 12, but is income from services taxable under either Article 14 (Independent Personal Services) or Article 15 (Dependent Personal Services). Professional services may be embodied in property that gives rise to royalties, however. Thus, if a professional contracts to develop patentable property and retains rights in the resulting property under the development contract, subsequent license payments made for those rights would be royalties.

*Paragraph 3*

This paragraph provides an exception to the rule of paragraph 1 that gives the state of residence exclusive taxing jurisdiction in cases where the beneficial owner of the royalties carries on business through a permanent establishment in the state of source or performs independent personal services from a fixed base situated in that state and the royalties are attributable to that permanent establishment or fixed base. In such cases the provisions of Article 7 (Business Profits) or Article 14 (Independent Personal Services) will apply.

The provisions of paragraph 4 of the Protocol apply to this paragraph. For example, royalty income that is attributable to a permanent establishment or a fixed base and that accrues during the existence of the permanent establishment or fixed base, but is received after the permanent establishment or fixed base no longer exists, remains taxable under the provisions of Articles 7 (Business Profits) or 14 (Independent Personal Services), respectively, and not under this Article.

*Paragraph 4*

Paragraph 4 provides that in cases involving special relationships between the payor and beneficial owner of royalties, Article 12 applies only to the extent the royalties would have been paid absent such special relationships (i.e., an arm's-length royalty). Any excess amount of royalties paid remains taxable according to the laws of the two Contracting States with due regard to the other provisions of the Convention. If, for example, the excess amount is treated as a distribution of corporate profits under domestic law, such excess amount will be taxed as a dividend rather than as royalties, but the tax imposed on the dividend payment will be subject to the rate limitations of paragraph 2 of Article 10 (Dividends).

*Paragraph 5*

Paragraph 5 is not found in the U.S. or OECD Models. It limits the extent to which one State may tax royalties paid by a resident of the other State. Subparagraphs (a) and (b) of paragraph 5 permit taxation of such royalties when they are paid to a resident of the first-mentioned State (subparagraph (a)), or when they are attributable to a permanent establishment or fixed base situated in that first-mentioned State (subparagraph (b)). Even without these two subparagraphs, these taxing rights could be exercised under the Convention by the State of residence of the State in which the permanent establishment or fixed base is located, under the saving clause of paragraph 4 of Article 1 (General Scope), Article 7 (Business Profits) or Article 15 (Independent Personal Services).

Subparagraphs (c) and (d) deal with taxation by one State of a royalty paid by a resident of the other State to a resident of a third State for the use of an intangible in the first-mentioned State. Subparagraph (c) provides that if a royalty is borne by a permanent establishment or fixed base located in one of the States, and the contract in connection with which the royalty was paid was concluded in connection with that permanent establishment or fixed base, the State where the permanent establishment or fixed base is located may tax the royalty if it is not paid to a resident of the other State. The rate of the tax imposed on the royalty may be limited by reference to the tax treaty, if any, in force between the taxing State and the third State. Thus, for example, if a new process is developed by a Canadian company and licensed for use in the United States by a U.S. permanent establishment of an Irish company, assuming that the royalties are paid by the branch, and deducted by it for U.S. tax purposes, then under U.S. law the Irish resident (*i.e.* the U.S. permanent establishment) is required to withhold U.S. tax on the royalty at a 10 percent rate, the rate applicable to royalties under the U.S.-Canada treaty. This result would also obtain absent the explicit statement in subparagraph 5(c) because the royalty is U.S. source under U.S. law, and it is not covered by the exemption in paragraph 1 of Article 12 since it would not be beneficially owned by a Irish resident.

Subparagraph (d) provides an additional case in which a State may tax royalties paid by a resident of the other state to a third-country resident. Under Code section 861(a)(4), and implicitly under the U.S. Model, any royalty paid for the use of an intangible in the United States, regardless of the residence of the payor, is U.S. source, which, subject to any limitations in the tax treaty, if any, between the United States and the country of residence of the beneficial owner, may be taxed by the United States. Under the Convention, however, in addition to the circumstances described in subparagraph (c), one State may tax a royalty paid by a resident of the other State only if (1) it is for the use of a property in the first-mentioned State, (2) it is not paid to a resident of that other State, (3) the payor of the royalty has also received a royalty in respect of the use of a property in the first-mentioned State, and that royalty is either paid by a resident of that first-mentioned State or borne by a permanent establishment or fixed base situated in that State, and (4) the use of the intangible is not a component part of or directly related to the active conduct of a trade or business in which the payor (*i.e.* the resident of the other State) is engaged. The last requirement is to be interpreted in accordance with paragraph 3 of Article 23 (Limitation on Benefits). For example, a Canadian resident licenses a patent for a process used in the automotive industry to a resident of Ireland, who in turn sub-licenses the patent to an automobile producer in the United States. The U.S. producer pays a royalty to the resident of Ireland for the use of the patent in the United States, and the Irish resident, in turn, pays a royalty to the Canadian resident for that same U.S. use of the patent. The royalty paid by the Irish resident to the resident of Canada would be exempt from U.S. tax under the provisions of paragraph 1 of Article 12. The royalty paid by the Irish resident to the resident of Canada, however, would be subject to U.S. tax under subparagraph (d). The rate would be set at 10 percent, under the provisions of the U.S.-Canada treaty. If, on the other hand, the Irish resident was also engaged in automobile production, the royalty paid by the Irish resident to the Canadian resident would not be subject to U.S. taxation.

*Relation to Other Articles*

Notwithstanding the foregoing limitations on source country taxation of royalties, the saving clause of paragraph 4 of Article 1 (General Scope) permits the United States to tax its residents and citizens, subject to the special foreign tax credit rules of paragraph 3 of Article 24 (Relief from Double Taxation), as if the Convention had not come into force.

As with other benefits of the Convention, the benefits of exclusive residence State taxation of royalties under paragraph 1 of Article 12 are available to a resident of the other State only if that resident is entitled to those benefits under Article 23 (Limitation on Benefits).

## Article 13 (Capital Gains)

Article 13 assigns either primary or exclusive taxing jurisdiction over gains from the alienation of property to the State of residence or the State of source and defines the terms necessary to apply the Article.

*Paragraph 1*

Paragraph 1 of Article 13 preserves the non-exclusive right of the State of source to tax gains attributable to the alienation of real property situated in that State. The paragraph therefore permits the United States to apply section 897 of the Code to tax gains derived by a resident of the other Contracting State that are attributable to the alienation of real property situated in the United States (as defined in paragraph 2). Gains attributable to the alienation of real property include gain from any other property that is treated as a real property interest within the meaning of paragraph 2. Although Ireland uses the term "immovable property", it is to be understood from the parenthetical use of "real property" that the two terms are synonymous.

*Paragraph 2*

This paragraph identifies the real property, gains from which are subject to the rule of paragraph 1. It includes real property referred to in Article 6 (i.e., an interest in the real property itself), a "United States real property interest" (when the United States is the other Contracting State under paragraph 1), and an equivalent interest in real property situated in Ireland. The OECD Model does not refer to real property interests other than the real property itself, and the United States has entered a reservation on this point with respect to the OECD Model, reserving the right to apply its tax under FIRPTA to all real estate gains encompassed by that provision.

Under section 897(c) of the Code the term "United States real property interest" includes shares in a U.S. corporation that owns sufficient U.S. real property interests to satisfy an asset-ratio test on certain testing dates. The term also includes certain foreign corporations that have elected to be treated as US corporations for this purpose. Section 897(i). In applying paragraph 1 the United States will look through distributions made by a REIT. Accordingly, distributions made by a REIT are taxable under paragraph 1 of Article 13 (not under Article 10 (Dividends)) when they are attributable to gains derived from the alienation of real property.

*Paragraph 3*

Paragraph 3 of Article 13 deals with the taxation of certain gains from the alienation of movable property forming part of the business property of a permanent establishment that an enterprise of a Contracting State has in the other Contracting State or of movable property pertaining to a fixed base available to a resident of a Contracting State in the other Contracting State for the purpose of performing independent personal services. This also includes gains from the alienation of such a permanent establishment (alone or with the whole enterprise) or of such fixed base. Such gains may be taxed in the State in which the permanent establishment or fixed base is located.

A resident of the other Contracting State that is a partner in a partnership doing business in the United States generally will have a permanent establishment in the United States as a result of the activities of the partnership, assuming that the activities of the partnership rise to the level of a permanent establishment. Rev. Rul. 91-32, 1991-1 C.B. 107. Further, under paragraph 3, the United States generally may tax a partner's distributive share of income realized by a partnership on the disposition of movable property forming part of the business property of the partnership in the United States.

In the case of a permanent establishment or fixed base that once existed in a Contracting State but that no longer exists, the provisions of paragraph 3 also apply, by virtue of paragraph 4 of the Protocol, to gain that would be attributable to such permanent establishment or fixed base if it did exist in the year of payment or accrual.

*Paragraph 4*

This paragraph limits the taxing jurisdiction of the state of source with respect to gains from the alienation of ships, aircraft, or containers operated in international traffic or movable property pertaining to the operation of such ships, aircraft, or containers. Under paragraph 4 when such income is derived by an enterprise of a Contracting State it is taxable only in that Contracting State. Notwithstanding paragraph 3, the rules of this paragraph apply even if the income is attributable to a permanent establishment maintained by the enterprise in the other Contracting State. This result is consistent with the general rule under Article 8 (Shipping and Air Transport) that confers exclusive taxing rights over international shipping and air transport income on the state of residence of the enterprise deriving such income.

*Paragraph 5*

Paragraph 5 grants to the State of residence of the alienator the exclusive right to tax gains from the alienation of property other than property referred to in paragraphs 1 through 4. For example, gain derived from shares, other than shares described in paragraphs 2 or 3, debt instruments and various financial instruments, may be taxed only in the State of residence, to the extent such income is not otherwise characterized as income taxable under another article (e.g., Article 10 (Dividends) or Article 11 (Interest)). Similarly gain derived from the alienation of tangible personal property, other than tangible personal property described in paragraph 3, may be taxed only in the State of residence of the alienator. Gain derived from the alienation of any property, such as a patent or copyright, that produces income taxable under Article 12 (Royalties) is taxable under Article 12 and not under this article, provided that such gain is of the type described in paragraph 2(b) of Article 12 (i.e., it is contingent on the productivity, use, or disposition of the property). Thus, under either article such gain is taxable only in the State of residence of the alienator. Sales by a resident of a Contracting State of real property located in a third state are not taxable in the other Contracting State, even if the sale is attributable to a permanent establishment located in the other Contracting State.

*Relation to Other Articles*

Notwithstanding the foregoing limitations on taxation of certain gains by the State of source, the saving clause of paragraph 4 of Article 1 (General Scope) permits the United States to tax its citizens and residents as if the Convention had not come into effect. Thus, any limitation in this Article on the right of the United States to tax gains does not apply to gains of a U.S. citizen or resident. The benefits of this Article are also subject to the provisions of Article 23 (Limitation on Benefits). Thus, only a resident of a Contracting State that satisfies one of the conditions in Article 23 is entitled to the benefits of this Article.

## Article 14 (Independent Personal Services)

The Convention deals in separate articles with different classes of income from personal services. Article 14 deals with the general class of income from independent personal services and Article 15 deals with the general class of income from dependent personal services. Articles 16 through 20 provide exceptions and additions to these general rules for directors' fees (Article 16); performance income of artistes and sportsmen (Article 17); pensions in respect of personal service income, social security benefits, annuities, alimony, and child support payments (Article 18); government service salaries and pensions (Article 19); and certain income of students and trainees (Article 20).

*Paragraph 1*

Paragraph 1 of Article 14 provides the general rule that an individual who is a resident of a Contracting State and who derives income from performing professional services or other activities of an independent character will be exempt from tax in respect of that income by the other Contracting State. The income may be taxed in the other Contracting State only if the services are performed there and the income is attributable to a fixed base that is regularly available to the individual in that other State for the purpose of performing his services. Like the U.S. Model, paragraph 7 of the Protocol states that the income taxable under Article 14 shall be determined under the principles of paragraph 3 of Article 7. Thus, all relevant expenses, including expenses not incurred in the Contracting State where the fixed base is located, must be allowed as deductions in computing the net income from services subject to tax in the Contracting State where the fixed base is located.

Income derived by persons other than individuals or groups of individuals from the performance of independent personal services is not covered by Article 14. Such income generally would be business profits taxable in accordance with Article 7 (Business Profits). Income derived by employees of such persons generally would be taxable in accordance with Article 15 (Dependent Personal Services).

The term "fixed base" is not defined in the Convention, but its meaning is understood to be similar, but not identical, to that of the term "permanent establishment," as defined in Article 5 (Permanent Establishment). The term "regularly available" also is not defined in the Convention. Whether a fixed base is regularly available to a person will be determined based on all the facts and circumstances. In general, the term encompasses situations where a fixed base is at the disposal of the individual whenever he performs services in that State. It is not necessary that the individual regularly use the fixed base, only that the fixed base be regularly available to him. For example, a U.S. resident partner in a law firm that has offices in Ireland would be considered to have a fixed base regularly available to him in Ireland if the law firm had an office in Ireland that was available to him whenever he wished to conduct business in Ireland, regardless of how frequently he conducted business in Ireland. On the other hand, an individual who had no office in Ireland and occasionally rented a hotel room to serve as a temporary office would not be considered to have a fixed base regularly available to him.

It is not necessary that the individual actually use the fixed base. It is only necessary that the fixed base be regularly available to him. For example, if an individual has an office in the other State that he can use if he chooses when he is present in the other State, that fixed base will be considered to be regularly available to him regardless of whether he conducts his activities there.

This Article applies to income derived by a partner resident in the Contracting State that is attributable to personal services of an independent character performed in the other State through a partnership that has a fixed base in that other Contracting State. Income which may be taxed under this Article includes all income attributable to the fixed base in respect of the performance of the personal services carried on by the partnership (whether by the partner himself, other partners in the partnership, or by employees assisting the partners) and any income from activities ancillary to the performance of those services (for example, charges for facsimile services). Income that is not derived from the performance of personal services and that is not ancillary thereto (for example, rental income from subletting office space), will be governed by other Articles of the Convention.

The application of Article 14 to a service partnership may be illustrated by the following example: a partnership formed in the Contracting State has five partners (who agree to split profits equally), four of whom are resident and perform personal services only in the Contracting State at Office A, and one of whom performs personal services from Office B, a fixed base in the other State. In this case, the four partners of the partnership resident in the Contracting State may be taxed in the other State in respect of their share of the income attributable to the fixed base, Office B. The services giving rise to income which may be attributed to the fixed base would include not only the services performed by the one resident partner, but also, for example, if one of the four other partners came to the other State and worked on an Office B matter there, the income in respect of those services also. As noted above, this would be the case regardless of whether the partner from the Contracting State actually visited or used Office B when performing services in the other State.

Paragraph 4 of the Protocol refers to Article 14. That rule clarifies that income that is attributable to a permanent establishment or a fixed base, but that is deferred and received after the permanent establishment or fixed base no longer exists, may nevertheless be taxed by the State in which the permanent establishment or fixed base was located. Thus, under Article 14, income derived by an individual resident of a Contracting State from services performed in the other Contracting State and attributable to a fixed base there may be taxed by that other State even if the income is deferred and received after there is no longer a fixed base available to the resident in that other State.

*Paragraph 2*

Paragraph 2, which follows the OECD Model, notes that the term "professional services" includes independent scientific, literary, artistic, educational or teaching activities, as well as the independent activities of physicians, lawyers, engineers, architects, dentists, and accountants. That list, however, is not exhaustive. The term includes all personal services performed by an individual for his own account, whether as a sole proprietor or a partner, where he receives the income and bears the risk of loss arising from the services. The taxation of income of an individual from those types of independent services which are covered by Articles 16 through 20 is governed by the provisions of those articles. For example, taxation of the income of a professional musician would be governed by Article 17 (Artistes and Athletes) rather than Article 14.

*Relation to Other Articles*

If an individual resident of Ireland who is also a U.S. citizen performs independent personal services in the United States, the United States may, by virtue of the saving clause of paragraph 4 of Article 1 (General Scope) tax his income without regard to the restrictions of this Article, subject to the special foreign tax credit rules of paragraph 3 of Article 24 (Relief from Double Taxation).

**Article 15 (Dependent Personal Services)**

Article 15 apportions taxing jurisdiction over remuneration derived by a resident of a Contracting State as an employee between the States of source and residence.

*Paragraph 1*

The general rule of Article 15 is contained in paragraph 1. Remuneration derived by a resident of a Contracting State as an employee may be taxed by the State of residence, and the remuneration also may be taxed by the other Contracting State to the extent derived from employment exercised (i.e., services performed) in the other Contracting State. Paragraph 1 also provides that the more specific rules of Articles 16 (Directors' Fees), 18 (Pensions, Social Security, Annuities, Alimony and Child Support), and 19 (Government Service) apply in the case of employment income described in one of these articles. Thus, even though the State of source has a right to tax employment income under Article 15, it may not have the right to tax that income under the Convention if the income is described, e.g., in Article 18 (Pensions, Social Security, Annuities, Alimony and Child Support) and is not taxable in the State of source under the provisions of that article.

Like the OECD Model, Article 15 of the Convention applies to "salaries, wages and other similar remuneration." Although the U.S. Model deletes the word "similar", this is meant merely as a clarification that Article 15 applies to any form of compensation for employment, including payments in kind, regardless of whether the remuneration is "similar" to salaries and wages.

Consistently with section 864(c)(6), Article 15 also applies regardless of the timing of actual payment for services. Thus, a bonus paid to a resident of a Contracting State with respect to services performed in the other Contracting State with respect to a particular taxable year would be subject to Article 15 for that year even if it was paid after the close of the year. Similarly, an annuity received for services performed in a taxable year would be subject to Article 15 despite the fact that it was paid in subsequent years. In either case, whether such payments were taxable in the State where the employment was exercised would depend on whether the tests of paragraph 2 were satisfied. Consequently, a person who receives the right to a future payment in consideration for services rendered in a Contracting State would be taxable in that State even if the payment is received at a time when the recipient is a resident of the other Contracting State.

*Paragraph 2*

Paragraph 2 sets forth an exception to the general rule that employment income may be taxed in the State where it is exercised. Under paragraph 2, the State where the employment is exercised may not tax the income from the employment if three conditions are satisfied: (a) the individual is present in the other Contracting State for a period or periods not exceeding 183 days in any 12-month period that begins or ends during the relevant (i.e., the year in which the services are performed) calendar year; (b) the remuneration is paid by, or on behalf of, an employer who is not a resident of that other Contracting State; and (c) the remuneration is not borne as a deductible expense by a permanent establishment or fixed base that the employer has in that other

State. In order for the remuneration to be exempt from tax in the source State, all three conditions must be satisfied. This exception is identical to that set forth in the U.S. and OECD Models.

The 183-day period in condition (a) is to be measured using the "days of physical presence" method. Under this method, the days that are counted include any day in which a part of the day is spent in the host country. (Rev. Rul. 56-24, 1956-1 C.B. 851.) Thus, days that are counted include the days of arrival and departure; weekends and holidays on which the employee does not work but is present within the country; vacation days spent in the country before, during or after the employment period, unless the individual's presence before or after the employment can be shown to be independent of his presence there for employment purposes; and time during periods of sickness, training periods, strikes, etc., when the individual is present but not working. If illness prevented the individual from leaving the country in sufficient time to qualify for the benefit, those days will not count. Also, any part of a day spent in the host country while in transit between two points outside the host country is not counted. These rules are consistent with the description of the 183-day period in paragraph 5 of the Commentary to Article 15 in the OECD Model.

Conditions (b) and (c) are intended to ensure that a Contracting State will not be required to allow a deduction to the payor for compensation paid and at the same time to exempt the employee on the amount received. Accordingly, if a foreign person pays the salary of an employee who is employed in the host State, but a host State corporation or permanent establishment reimburses the payor with a payment that can be identified as a reimbursement, neither condition (b) nor (c), as the case may be, will be considered to have been fulfilled.

The reference to remuneration "borne by" a permanent establishment or fixed base is understood to encompass all expenses that economically are incurred and not merely expenses that are currently deductible for tax purposes. Accordingly, the expenses referred to include expenses that are capitalizable as well as those that are currently deductible. Further, salaries paid by residents that are exempt from income taxation may be considered to be borne by a permanent establishment or fixed base notwithstanding the fact that the expenses will be neither deductible nor capitalizable since the payor is exempt from tax.

*Paragraph 3*

Paragraph 3 contains a special rule applicable to remuneration for services performed by a resident of a Contracting State as an employee aboard a ship or aircraft operated in international traffic. Such remuneration may be taxed only in the State of residence of the employee if the services are performed as a member of the regular complement of the ship or aircraft. The "regular complement" includes the crew. In the case of a cruise ship, for example, it may also include others, such as entertainers, lecturers, etc., employed by the shipping company to serve on the ship throughout its voyage. The use of the term "regular complement" is intended to clarify that a person who exercises his employment as, for example, an insurance salesman while aboard a ship or aircraft is not covered by this paragraph. This paragraph is inapplicable to persons dealt with in Article 14 (Independent Personal Services).

The comparable paragraph in the OECD Model provides that such income may be taxed (on a non-exclusive basis) in the Contracting State in which the place of effective management of the employing enterprise is situated. The Convention, like the U.S. Model, does not adopt this rule because the United States exercises its taxing jurisdiction over an employee only if the employee is a U.S. citizen or resident, or the services are performed by the employee in the United States. Tax cannot be imposed simply because an employee works for an enterprise that is a resident of the United States. The U.S. Model ensures that, given U.S. law, each employee will be subject to one level of tax.

*Relation to Other Articles*

If a U.S. citizen who is resident in Ireland performs services as an employee in the United States and meets the conditions of paragraph 2 for source country exemption, he nevertheless is taxable in the United States by virtue of the saving clause of paragraph 4 of Article 1 (General Scope), subject to the special foreign tax credit rule of paragraph 3 of Article 24 (Relief from Double Taxation).

## Article 16 (Directors' Fees)

This Article provides that directors' fees and other similar payments derived by a resident of a Contracting State in his capacity as a member of the board of directors of a company resident in the other Contracting State may be taxed in the State where the income arises. Such income will be deemed to arise in the Contracting State in which the company is resident except to the extent that such fees are paid in respect of attendance at meetings held in the State of residence of the director. So, for example, if a U.S. resident receives annual compensation for performing his duties as a director of an Irish company, and all of the company's board meetings are held outside the United States (whether in Ireland or elsewhere), all of the compensation would be deemed to arise in, and therefore could be taxed by, Ireland. If, however, the director attended any meetings in the United States, any amount received with respect to attendance at such meetings would be deemed to arise in the United States, and therefore would be taxable only in the United States. The result under this rule is similar to that under the OECD Model provision, but differs from the U.S. Model, under which the State of residence of the corporation may tax nonresident directors with no time or dollar threshold, but only with respect to remuneration for services actually performed in that State.

The rule of Article 16 is an exception to the more general rules of Article 14 (Independent Personal Services) and Article 15 (Dependent Personal Services). Thus, for example, in determining whether a director's fee paid to a non-employee director is subject to tax in the country of residence of the corporation, it is not relevant to establish whether the fee is attributable to a fixed base in that State.

*Relation to Other Articles*

The sourcing rule in paragraph 2 of this Article is exempt from the saving clause of paragraph 4 of Article 1 (General Scope) by reason of subparagraph 5(a) of Article 1. For example, if a U.S. resident is a director of an Irish company, the United States must treat the fees received by that resident in his capacity as a director as Irish source income, except to the extent that those fees are paid in respect of attendance at a board meeting held in the United States. Thus, fees that may be attributable to the director's services performed within the United States but that are not paid in respect of meetings held in the United States would be treated as U.S. source income under the Code but are treated as Irish source income under the Convention for purposes of applying the foreign tax credit limitations of section 904 of the Code.

## Article 17 (Artistes and Sportsmen)

This Article deals with the taxation in a Contracting State of artistes (i.e., performing artists and entertainers) and sportsmen resident in the other Contracting State from the performance of their services as such. The Article applies both to the income of an entertainer or sportsman who performs services on his own behalf and one who performs services on behalf of another person, either as an employee of that person, or pursuant to any other arrangement. The rules of this Article take precedence, in some circumstances, over those of Articles 14 (Independent Personal Services) and 15 (Dependent Personal Services).

This Article applies only with respect to the income of performing artists and sportsmen. Others involved in a performance or athletic event, such as producers, directors, technicians, managers, coaches, etc., remain subject to the provisions of Articles 14 and 15. In addition, except as provided in paragraph 2, income earned by juridical persons is not covered by Article 17.

*Paragraph 1*

Paragraph 1 describes the circumstances in which a Contracting State may tax the performance income of an entertainer or sportsman who is a resident of the other Contracting State. Under the paragraph, income derived by an individual resident of a Contracting State from activities as an entertainer or sportsman exercised in the other Contracting State may be taxed in that other State if the amount of the gross receipts derived by the performer exceeds $20,000 (or its equivalent in Irish pounds) for the taxable year. The $20,000 includes expenses reimbursed to the individual or borne on his behalf. If the gross receipts exceed $20,000, the full amount, not just the excess, may be taxed in the State of performance.

The OECD Model provides for taxation by the country of performance of the remuneration of entertainers or sportsmen with no dollar or time threshold. This treaty introduces the dollar threshold test to distinguish between two groups of entertainers and athletes -- those who are paid very large sums of money for very short periods of service, and who would, therefore, normally be exempt from host country tax under the standard personal services income rules, and those who earn relatively modest amounts and are, therefore, not easily distinguishable from those who earn other types of personal service income. The United States has entered a reservation to the OECD Model on this point.

Tax may be imposed under paragraph 1 even if the performer would have been exempt from tax under Articles 14 (Independent Personal Services) or 15 (Dependent Personal Services). On the other hand, if the performer would be exempt from host-country tax under Article 17, but would be taxable under either Article 14 or 15, tax may be imposed under either of those Articles. Thus, for example, if a performer derives remuneration from his activities in an independent capacity, and the remuneration is not attributable to a fixed base, he may be taxed by the host State in accordance with Article 17 if his remuneration exceeds $20,000 annually, despite the fact that he generally would be exempt from host State taxation under Article 14. However, a performer who receives less than the $20,000 threshold amount and therefore is not taxable under Article 17, nevertheless may be subject to tax in the host country under Articles 14 or 15 if the tests for host-country taxability under those Articles are met. For example, if an entertainer who is an independent contractor earns $19,000 of income in a State for the calendar year, but the income is attributable to a fixed base regularly available to him in the State of performance, that State may tax his income under Article 14. This interpretation is consistent with the prevailing understanding under Article 17 of other U.S. tax treaties, but has been clarified by amendments to the text of paragraph 1 in the U.S. Model and this Convention.

Since it frequently is not possible to know until year-end whether the income an entertainer or sportsman derived from a performance in a Contracting State will exceed $20,000, nothing in the Convention precludes that Contracting State from withholding tax during the year and refunding after the close of the year if the taxability threshold has not been met.

Article 17 applies to all income connected with a performance by the entertainer, such as appearance fees, award or prize money, and a share of the gate receipts. This interpretation is consistent with paragraph 9 of the OECD Commentaries on Article 17. Income derived from a Contracting State by a performer who is a resident of the other Contracting State from other than actual performance, such as royalties from record sales and payments for product endorsements, is not covered by this Article, but by other articles of the Convention, such as Article 12 (Royalties) or Article 14 (Independent Personal Services). For example, if an entertainer receives royalty income from the sale of live recordings, the royalty income would be exempt from source country tax under Article 12, even if the performance was conducted in the source country, although he could be taxed in the source country with respect to income from the performance itself under this Article if the dollar threshold is exceeded.

In determining whether income falls under Article 17 or another article, the controlling factor will be whether the income in question is predominantly attributable to the performance itself or other activities or property rights. For instance, a fee paid to a performer for endorsement of a performance in which the performer will participate would be considered to be so closely associated with the performance itself that it normally would fall within Article 17. Similarly, a sponsorship fee paid by a business in return for the right to attach its name to the performance would be so closely associated with the performance that it would fall under Article 17 as well. As indicated in paragraph 9 of the Commentaries to Article 17 of the OECD Model, a cancellation fee would not be considered to fall within Article 17 but would be dealt with under Article 7, 14 or 15.

As explained in paragraph 4 of the Commentaries to Article 17 of the OECD Model, where an individual fulfills a dual role as performer and non-performer (such as a player-coach or an actor-director), but his role in one of the two capacities is negligible, the predominant character of the individual's activities should control the characterization of those activities. In other cases there should be an apportionment between the performance-related compensation and other compensation.

Consistently with Article 15 (Dependent Personal Services), Article 17 also applies regardless of the timing of actual payment for services. Thus, a bonus paid to a resident of a Contracting State with respect to a performance in the other Contracting State with respect to a particular taxable year would be subject to Article 17 for that year even if it was paid after the close of the year.

*Paragraph 2*

Paragraph 2 is intended to deal with the potential for abuse when a performer's income does not accrue directly to the performer himself, but to another person. Foreign performers commonly perform in the United States as employees of, or under contract with, a company or other person.

The relationship may truly be one of employee and employer, with no abuse of the tax system either intended or realized. On the other hand, the "employer" may, for example, be a company established and owned by the performer, which is merely acting as the nominal income recipient in respect of the remuneration for the performance (a "star company"). The performer may act as an "employee," receive a modest salary, and arrange to receive the remainder of the income from his performance in another form or at a later time. In such case, absent the provisions of paragraph 2, the income arguably could escape host-country tax because the recipient earns business profits but has no permanent establishment in that country. The performer may largely or entirely escape host-country tax by receiving only a small salary in the year the services are performed, perhaps small enough to place him below the dollar threshold in paragraph 1. The performer might arrange to receive further payments in a later year, when he is not subject to host-country tax, perhaps as deferred salary payments, dividends or liquidating distributions.

Paragraph 2 seeks to prevent this type of abuse while at the same time protecting the taxpayers' rights to the benefits of the Convention when there is a legitimate employee-employer relationship between the performer and the person providing his services. Under paragraph 2, when the income accrues to a person other than the performer, and the performer or related persons participate, directly or indirectly, in the receipts or profits of that other person, the income may be taxed in the Contracting State where the performer's services are exercised, without regard to the provisions of the Convention concerning business profits (Article 7) or independent personal services (Article 14). Thus, even if the "employer" has no permanent establishment or fixed base in the host country, its income may be subject to tax there under the provisions of paragraph 2. Taxation under paragraph 2 is on the person providing the services of the performer. This paragraph does not affect the rules of paragraph 1, which apply to the performer himself. The income taxable by virtue of paragraph 2 is reduced to the extent of salary payments to the performer, which fall under paragraph 1.

For purposes of paragraph 2, income is deemed to accrue to another person (i.e., the person providing the services of the performer) if that other person has control over, or the right to receive, gross income in respect of the services of the performer. Direct or indirect participation in the profits of a person may include, but is not limited to, the accrual or receipt of deferred remuneration, bonuses, fees, dividends, partnership income or other income or distributions.

Paragraph 2 does not apply if it is established that neither the performer nor any persons related to the performer participate directly or indirectly in the receipts or profits of the person providing the services of the performer. Assume, for example, that a circus owned by a U.S. corporation performs in Ireland, and promoters of the performance in Ireland pay the circus, which, in turn, pays salaries to the circus performers. The circus is determined to have no permanent establishment in Ireland. Since the circus performers do not participate in the profits of the circus, but merely receive their salaries out of the circus' gross receipts, the circus is protected by Article 7 and its income is not subject to host-country tax. Whether the salaries of the circus performers are subject to host-country tax under this Article depends on whether they exceed the $20,000 threshold in paragraph 1.

Since pursuant to Article 1 (General Scope) the Convention only applies to persons who are residents of one of the Contracting States, if the star company is not a resident of one of the Contracting States, then taxation of the income is not affected by Article 17 or any other provision of the Convention.

This exception from paragraph 2 for non-abusive cases is not found in the OECD Model. The United States has entered a reservation to the OECD Model on this point.

*Relationship to other articles*

This Article is subject to the provisions of the saving clause of paragraph 4 of Article 1 (General Scope). Thus, if an entertainer or a sportsman who is resident in Ireland is a citizen of the United States, the United States may tax all of his income from performances in the United States without regard to the provisions of this Article, subject, however, to the special foreign tax credit provisions of paragraph 3 of Article 24 (Relief from Double Taxation). In addition, benefits of this Article are subject to the provisions of Article 23 (Limitation on Benefits).

## Article 18 (Pensions, Social Security, Annuities, Alimony and Child Support)

This Article deals with the taxation of private (i.e., non-government service) pensions and annuities, social security benefits, alimony and child support payments and with the tax treatment of contributions to pension plans.

*Subparagraph 1 (a)*

Subparagraph 1 (a) provides that pensions and other similar remuneration derived and beneficially owned by a resident of a Contracting State in consideration of past employment are taxable only in the State of residence of the beneficiary. Although the Convention does not make explicit the fact that the term "pensions and other similar remuneration" includes both periodic and single sum payments, it is understood that this would be the case under the domestic law of both Contracting States. The treatment of such payments under the Convention is essentially the ame as under the 1951 Convention. The term "pensions and other similar remuneration" is intended to encompass payments made by all private retirement plans and arrangements in consideration of past employment, regardless of whether they are qualified plans under U.S. law, including plans and arrangements described in section 457 or 414(d) of the Internal Revenue Code. It also includes an Individual Retirement Account.

Pensions in respect of government service are not covered by this paragraph. They are covered either by subparagraph 1 (b) of this Article, if they are in the form of social security benefits, or by paragraph 2 of Article 19 (Government Service). Thus, Article 19 covers section 457, 401(a) and 403(b) plans established for government employees. If a pension in respect of government service is not covered by Article 19 solely because the services were rendered in connection with a business, the pension is covered by this Article.

*Subparagraph 1(b)*

The treatment of social security benefits is dealt with in subparagraph 1(b). This subparagraph provides that payments made by one of the Contracting States under the provisions of its social security or similar legislation to a resident of the other Contracting State will be taxable only in the other Contracting State. This subparagraph applies to social security beneficiaries whether they have contributed to the system as private sector or Government employees.

The reference to "provisions of the social security" legislation is not restricted to old age pensions but refers to all sorts of social security benefits, including benefits granted in kind and payments made as compensation for work-related diseases or accidents. Paragraph 2 of the diplomatic notes explains that the phrase "similar legislation" is intended to refer to United States tier 1 Railroad Retirement benefits.

*Paragraph 2*

Under paragraph 2, annuities that are derived and beneficially owned by a resident of a Contracting State are taxable only in that State. An annuity, as the term is used in this paragraph, means a stated sum paid periodically at stated times during a specified number of years or for life, under an obligation to make the payment in return for adequate and full consideration (other than for services rendered). An annuity received in consideration for services rendered would be treated as deferred compensation and generally taxable in accordance with Article 15 (Dependent Personal Services).

*Paragraphs 3 and 4*

Paragraphs 3 and 4 deal with alimony and child support payments. Both alimony, under paragraph 3, and child support payments, under paragraph 4, are defined as periodic payments made pursuant to a written separation agreement or a decree of divorce, judicial separation, separate maintenance, or compulsory support. Paragraph 3, however, deals only with payments of that type that are deductible to the payor. Under that paragraph, alimony paid by a resident of a Contracting State to a resident of the other Contracting State is taxable under the Convention only in the State of residence of the recipient. Paragraph 4 deals with those periodic payments that are for the support of a child and that are not covered by paragraph 3 (i.e., those payments that are not deductible to the payor). These types of payments by a resident of a Contracting State to a resident of the other Contracting State may not be taxed by either Contracting State.

*Paragraphs 5 and 6*

Paragraphs 5 and 6 deals with cross-border pension contributions in order to remove barriers to the flow of personal services between the Contracting States that could otherwise result from a failure of the two Contracting States' laws regarding the deductibility of pension contributions to mesh properly. Many countries allow deductions or exclusions to their residents for contributions, made by them or on their behalf, to resident pension plans, but do not allow deductions or exclusions for payments made to plans resident in another country, even if the structure and legal requirements of such plans in the two countries are similar.

Paragraph 5 provides for deductions (or exclusions) from the taxable income of an individual in one State for contributions paid by that individual to a pension plan in the other State if certain conditions are satisfied. Paragraph 5 also provides that payments made to such a plan by or on behalf of the individual's employer are deductible from the profits of the employer in that State and are not considered part of the taxable income of the individual. The benefits granted by a State under this paragraph (i.e., the deductibility of contributions) are limited to the benefits allowed by that State to its own residents for contributions to a pension plan recognized for tax purposes by that State.

Where the United States is the host country, the exclusion of employee contributions from the employee's income under this paragraph is limited to elective contributions not in excess of the amount specified in section 402(g). Deduction of employer contributions is subject to the limitations of sections 415 and 404. The section 404 limitation on deductions would be calculated as if the individual were the only employee covered by the plan.

The benefits of this paragraph are allowed to an individual who is present in one of the Contracting States to perform either dependent or independent personal services. Subparagraph 5(a) provides that the individual can receive the benefits of this paragraph only if he was contributing to the plan in his home country, or to a similar plan that was replaced by the plan to which he is contributing, before coming to the host country. The allowance of a successor plan would apply if, for example, the employer has been taken over by another corporation that replaces the existing plan with its own plan, rolling membership in the old plan over into the new plan.

Subparagraph 5 (b) limits the duration of the benefit by restricting eligibility to individuals who have performed personal services in the host country for a cumulative period not exceeding five calendar years.

In addition, Subparagraph 5 (c) provides that the host-country competent authority must determine that the pension plan to which a contribution is made in the home country of the individual generally corresponds to a plan recognized for tax purposes in the host country. It is understood that United States plans eligible for the benefits of paragraph 5 include qualified plans under section 403(a), individual retirement plans (including individual retirement plans that are part of a simplified employee pension plan that satisfies section 408(k), IRAs and section 408(p) accounts), section 403(a) qualified annuity plans, individual retirement accounts, and section 403(b) plans.

The benefits under paragraph 5 are limited to the benefits that the host country accords, under its law, to the host country plan most similar to the home country plan, even if the home country would have afforded greater benefits under its law. Thus, for example, if the host country has a cap on contributions equal to, say, five percent of the remuneration, and the home country has a seven percent cap, the deduction is limited to five percent, even though if the individual had remained in his home country he would have been allowed to take the larger deduction.

*Paragraph 6*

Paragraph 6 is included in the Convention because Ireland continues to maintain a remittance system of taxation for individuals who are resident but not domiciled in Ireland. Such persons are subject to tax in Ireland on non-Irish source income only to the extent the income or chargeable gains are remitted to the Irish resident. Paragraph 6 limits the deductibility from an individual's taxable income provided under paragraph 5 for contributions to a foreign pension plan in cases in which the host State taxes only so much of that individual's income as is remitted to or received by the individual in that State. In such a case, the deduction that would otherwise be permitted under paragraph 5 is reduced by a proportion equal to the proportion of the individual's income that is untaxed in that State because it was not remitted to or received by the individual in that State.

Domicile is a legal concept that is not necessarily related to residence. An individual receives a domicile of origin at birth. The individual may change that domicile by physically relocating with the intention of changing his domicile.

*Relation to other Articles*

Paragraphs 1, 2, and 3 of Article 18 are subject to the saving clause of paragraph 4 of Article 1 (General Scope). Thus, a U.S. citizen who is resident in Ireland, and receives either a pension, social security, annuity or alimony payment from the United States, may be subject to U.S. tax on the payment, notwithstanding the rules in those three paragraphs that give the State of residence of the recipient the exclusive taxing right. Paragraph 4 is excepted from the saving clause by virtue of paragraph 5(a) of Article 1. Thus, the United States will allow U.S. citizens and residents the benefits of paragraph 4. By virtue of paragraph 5(b) of Article 1, paragraph 5 is excepted from the saving clause with respect to individuals who are residents of a Contracting State but are neither citizens nor permanent residents of that State.

**Article 19 (Government Service)**

*Paragraph 1*

Subparagraphs (a) and (b) of paragraph 1 deal with the taxation of government compensation (other than a pension addressed in paragraph 2). Subparagraph (a) provides that remuneration paid by one of the States or its political subdivisions or local authorities to any individual who is rendering services to that State, political subdivision or local authority is exempt from tax by the other State. Under subparagraph (b), such payments are, however, taxable exclusively in the other State (i.e., the host State) if the services are rendered in that other State and the individual is a resident of that State who is either a national of that State or a person who did not become resident of that State solely for purposes of rendering the services.

This paragraph follows the OECD Model, but differs from the U.S. Model, in applying only to government employees and not to independent contractors engaged by governments to perform services for them.

*Paragraph 2*

Paragraph 2 deals with the taxation of a pension paid by, or out of funds created by, one of the States or a political subdivision or a local authority thereof to an individual in respect of services rendered to that State or subdivision or authority. Subparagraph (a) provides that such a pension is taxable only in that State. Subparagraph (b) provides an exception under which such a pension is taxable only in the other State if the individual is a resident of, and a national of, that other State. Pensions paid to retired civilian and military employees of a Government of either State are intended to be covered under paragraph 2. When benefits paid by a State in respect of services rendered to that State or a subdivision or authority are in the form of social security benefits, however, those payments are covered by subparagraph 1(b) of Article 18 (Pensions, Social Security, Annuities, Alimony and Child Support). As a general matter, the result will differ depending upon whether Article 18 or 19 applies, since social security benefits are generally taxable exclusively by the residence country while government pensions are generally taxable exclusively by the source country. The result will be the same only when the payment is made to a citizen and resident of the other Contracting State, who is not also a citizen of the paying State. In such a case, government pensions become taxable only in the residence country and social security benefits continue to be taxable only in the residence country.

*Paragraph 3*

Paragraph 3 specifies that paragraphs 1 and 2 do not apply to remuneration and pensions paid for services performed in connection with a business carried on by a Contracting State or a political subdivision or local authority thereof. In such cases, the remuneration and pensions are subject instead to the provisions of Articles 14 (Independent Personal Services), 15 (Dependent Personal Services), 16 (Director's Fees), 17 (Artistes and Sportsmen), or 18 (Pensions, Social Security, Annuities, Alimony and Child Support). This language conforms to the OECD model.

## Article 20 (Students and Trainees)

This Article provides rules for host-country taxation of visiting students, apprentices or business trainees. Persons who meet the tests of the Article will be exempt from tax in the State that they are visiting with respect to designated classes of income. Several conditions must be satisfied in order for an individual to be entitled to the benefits of this Article.

First, the visitor must have been, either at the time of his arrival in the host State or immediately before, a resident of the other Contracting State.

Second, the purpose of the visit must be the full-time education or training of the visitor. Thus, if the visitor comes principally to work in the host State but also is a part-time student, he would not be entitled to the benefits of this Article, even with respect to any payments he may receive from abroad for his maintenance or education, and regardless of whether or not he is in a degree program. Whether a student is to be considered full-time will be determined by the rules of the educational institution at which he is studying. Similarly, a person who visits the host State for the purpose of obtaining business training and who also receives a salary from his employer for providing services would not be considered a trainee and would not be entitled to the benefits of this Article.

Third, a student must be studying at a recognized educational institution. (This requirement does not apply to business trainees or apprentices.) An educational institution is understood to be an institution that normally maintains a regular faculty and normally has a regular body of students in attendance at the place where the educational activities are carried on. An educational institution will be considered to be recognized if it is accredited by an authority that generally is responsible for accreditation of institutions in the particular field of study.

The host-country exemption in the Article applies only to payments received by the student, apprentice or business trainee for the purpose of his maintenance, education or training that arise outside the host State. A payment will be considered to arise outside the host State if the payor is located outside the host State. Thus, if an employer from the U.S. sends an employee to Ireland for training, the payments the trainee receives from abroad from his employer for his maintenance or training while he is present in the host State will be exempt from host-country tax. In all cases substance over form should prevail in determining the identity of the payor. Consequently, payments made directly or indirectly by the U.S. person with whom the visitor is training, but which have been routed through a non-host-country source, such as, for example, a foreign bank account, should not be treated as arising outside the United States for this purpose.

In the case of an apprentice or business trainee, the benefits of the Article will extend only for a period of one year from the time that the visitor first arrives in the host country. If, however, an apprentice or trainee remains in the host country for a second year, thus losing the benefits of the Article, he would not retroactively lose the benefits of the Article for the first year.

The saving clause of paragraph 4 of Article 1 (General Scope) does not apply to this Article with respect to an individual who is neither a citizen of the host State nor has been admitted for permanent residence there. The saving clause, however, does apply with respect to citizens and permanent residents of the host State. Thus, a U.S. citizen who is a resident of Ireland and who visits the United States as a full-time student at an accredited university will not be exempt from U.S. tax on remittances from abroad that otherwise constitute U.S. taxable income. A person, however, who is not a U.S. citizen, and who visits the United States as a student and remains long enough to become a resident under U.S. law, but does not become a permanent resident (i.e., does not acquire a green card), will be entitled to the full benefits of the Article.

## Article 21 (Offshore Exploration and Exploitation Activities)

This Article deals exclusively with the taxation of activities carried on by a resident of one of the Contracting States on the continental shelf of the other Contracting State in connection with the exploration or exploitation of the natural resources of the shelf, principally activities connected with exploration for oil by offshore drilling rigs. In the U.S. and OECD Models, the income from these activities is subject to the standard rules found in the other Articles of the Convention (e.g., the business profits and personal services articles). Other U.S. treaties with countries bordering on the North Sea (e.g., Norway, the United Kingdom and the Netherlands), however, have articles dealing with offshore activities. Several recent Irish treaties and the Irish model treaty also contain such provisions. The prior Convention had no similar provision. The normal business profits and personal services provisions, therefore, applied under the prior Convention to offshore income.

*Paragraph 1*

Paragraph 1 states that the provisions of Article 21 apply, notwithstanding any other provision of the Convention, to activities carried on offshore in connection with the exploration or exploitation of the sea bed and subsoil and their natural resources situated in a Contracting State. These activities are referred to as "exploration activities" and "exploitation activities" respectively. Although there are no explicit references to other articles, the implicit references are principally to Articles 5 (Permanent Establishment), 7 (Business Profits), 14 (Independent Personal Services) and 15 (Dependent Personal Services). For example, if a drilling rig of a U.S. enterprise is present on the continental shelf of Ireland for 10 months and would, therefore, not constitute a permanent establishment because of the 12-month construction site rule of paragraph 3 of Article 5, the rig would, nevertheless, be deemed to be a permanent establishment under paragraph 2 of this Article.

*Paragraphs 2 and 3*

Paragraphs 2 and 3 provide the basic rules for determining when an enterprise is deemed to have a permanent establishment as a result of offshore activities. The general rule is that all exploitation activities give rise to a permanent establishment, while exploration activities create a permanent establishment only if they continue for a period of 120 days in a twelve-month period.

Paragraph 2 provides that, subject to the exception of paragraph 3, an enterprise of one Contracting State carrying on exploration activities or exploitation activities in the other Contracting State will be deemed to be carrying on business through a permanent establishment situated there.

Paragraph 3 provides that an enterprise of a Contracting State carrying on exploration activities in the other Contracting State will not constitute a permanent establishment unless the activities are carried on there for a period or periods aggregating more than 120 days within any period of twelve months. Paragraph 3 also provides rules for aggregating the activities of related parties for purposes of determining whether the threshold has been met. If the enterprise carrying on the offshore activities is associated with another enterprise, and that associated enterprise is carrying on substantially similar exploration activities there, the former enterprise shall be deemed to be carrying on all such activities, except to the extent that those activities are carried on at the same time. For purposes of this rule, an enterprise is associated with another if one participates directly or indirectly in the management, control or capital of the other or if the same persons participate directly or indirectly in the management, control or capital of both enterprises.

Ireland agrees, in Paragraph 8 of the Protocol, to limit the "balancing charge" that otherwise would apply upon the cessation of offshore activities. Under Ireland's domestic law, a balancing charge may be levied upon the termination of a permanent establishment to tax deemed gain on the assets of the permanent establishment. Where a permanent establishment is deemed to exist by virtue of Article 21, the Protocol provision limits the balancing charge so that it is imposed only to the extent that the person carrying on the activities has claimed accelerated capital allowances (depreciation). Normal capital allowances would be allowed and would not be subject to recapture through a balancing charge. Since Ireland currently has no accelerated capital allowances, the Protocol provision currently prevents Ireland from imposing any balancing charges upon the termination of offshore activity where a permanent establishment is deemed to exist by virtue of Article 21.

*Paragraphs 4 and 5*

Paragraphs 4 and 5 provide thresholds with respect to offshore activities consisting of personal services that are similar to the thresholds in paragraphs 2 and 3. Paragraph 4 provides that income derived by a resident of a Contracting State carrying on exploitation activities in the other Contracting State that consist of professional services or other activities of an independent character will be deemed to be attributable to a fixed base in the other Contracting State. That is also true with respect to services of an independent character that constitute exploration activities, but only if the activities are performed in the other Contracting State for a period or periods in excess of 120 days within a twelve-month period.

Paragraph 5 contains the rules for the taxation of employment income connected with offshore activities. It provides for a broader host-country taxing right than does Article 15 (Dependent Personal Services). Under paragraph 5, salaries and other remuneration of a resident of one Contracting State derived from an employment in connection with offshore activities carried on through a permanent establishment in the other may be taxed by the other State. Paragraph 5 contains no special rule regarding the taxation of persons employed on ships, etc., in connection with offshore activities. Under Article 15, the presence of a permanent establishment is not sufficient to subject the employee to host country taxation. Under paragraph 5 of Article 21, however, an employee merely needs to be engaged in offshore activities carried on in connection with an Irish permanent establishment engaged in offshore activities in Ireland to be subject to tax, regardless of who pays his salary and whether it is deductible in Ireland, and regardless of the amount of time he has spent in, or off the shore of, Ireland.

*Relation to other Articles*

As with any benefit of the Convention, an enterprise or individual claiming a benefit under this Article must be entitled to the benefit under the provisions of Article 23 (Limitation on Benefits).

## Article 22 (Other Income)

Article 22 generally assigns taxing jurisdiction over income not dealt with in the other Articles (Articles 6 through 20) of the Convention to the State of residence of the beneficial owner of the income and defines the terms necessary to apply the article. An item of income is "dealt with" in another Article if it is the type of income described in the Article and it has its source in a Contracting State. For example, all royalty income that arises in a Contracting State and that is beneficially owned by a resident of the other Contracting State is "dealt with" in Article 12 (Royalties).

Examples of items of income covered by Article 22 include income from gambling, punitive (but not compensatory) damages, covenants not to compete, and income from certain financial instruments to the extent derived by persons not engaged in the trade or business of dealing in such instruments (unless the transaction giving rise to the income is related to a trade or business, in which case it is dealt with under Article 7 (Business Profits)). The Article also applies to items of income that are not dealt with in the other articles because of their source or some other characteristic. For example, Article 11 (Interest) addresses only the taxation of interest arising in a Contracting State. Interest arising in a third State that is not attributable to a permanent establishment, therefore, is subject to Article 22.

Distributions from partnerships and distributions from trusts are not generally dealt with under Article 22 because partnership and trust distributions generally do not constitute income. Under the Code, partners include in income their distributive share of partnership income annually, and partnership distributions themselves generally do not give rise to income. Also, under the Code, trust income and distributions have the character of the associated distributable net income and therefore would generally be covered by another article of the Convention. See Code section 641 et seq.

*Paragraph 1*

The general rule of Article 22 is contained in paragraph 1. Items of income not dealt with in other articles and beneficially owned by a resident of a Contracting State will be taxable only in the State of residence. This exclusive right of taxation applies whether or not the residence State exercises its right to tax the income covered by the Article.

This paragraph differs in one respect from the OECD Model, but is consistent with the current U.S. Model, by referring to "items of income beneficially owned by a resident of a Contracting State" rather than simply "items of income of a resident of a Contracting State." This is not a substantive change. It is intended merely to make explicit the implicit understanding in other treaties that the exclusive residence taxation provided by paragraph 1 applies only when a resident of a Contracting State is the beneficial owner of the income. This should also be understood from the phrase "income of a resident of a Contracting State." The addition of a reference to beneficial ownership merely removes any possible ambiguity. Thus, source taxation of income not dealt with in other articles of the Convention is not limited by paragraph 1 if it is nominally paid to a resident of the other Contracting State, but is beneficially owned by a resident of a third State.

*Paragraph 2*

This paragraph provides an exception to the general rule of paragraph 1 for income, other than income from real property, that is attributable to a permanent establishment or fixed base maintained in a Contracting State by a resident of the other Contracting State. The taxation of such income is governed by the provisions of Articles 7 (Business Profits) and 14 (Independent Personal Services). Therefore, income arising outside the United States that is attributable to a permanent establishment maintained in the United States by a resident of Ireland generally would be taxable by the United States under the provisions of Article 7. This would be true even if the income is sourced in a third State.

There is an exception to this general rule with respect to income a resident of a Contracting State derives from real property located outside the other Contracting State (whether in the first-mentioned Contracting State or in a third State) that is attributable to the resident's permanent establishment or fixed base in the other Contracting State. In such a case, only the first-mentioned Contracting State (i.e., the State of residence of the person deriving the income) and not the host State of the permanent establishment or fixed base may tax that income. This special rule for foreign-situs property is consistent with the general rule, also reflected in Article 6 (Income from Immovable Property (Real Property)), that only the situs and residence States may tax real property and real property income. Even if such property is part of the property of a permanent establishment or fixed base in a Contracting State, that State may not tax if neither the situs of the property nor the residence of the owner is in that State.

*Relation to Other Articles*

This Article is subject to the saving clause of paragraph 4 of Article 1 (General Scope). Thus, the United States may tax the income of a resident of Ireland that is not dealt with elsewhere in the Convention, if that resident is a citizen of the United States. The Article is also subject to the provisions of Article 23 (Limitation on Benefits). Thus, if a resident of Ireland earns income that falls within the scope of paragraph 1 of Article 22, but that is taxable by the

United States under U.S. law, the income would be exempt from U.S. tax under the provisions of Article 22 only if the resident satisfies one of the tests of Article 23 for entitlement to benefits.

## Article 23 (Limitation on Benefits)

*Purpose of Limitation on Benefits Provisions*

The United States views an income tax treaty as a vehicle for providing treaty benefits to residents of the two Contracting States. This statement begs the question of who is to be treated as a resident of a Contracting State for the purpose of being granted treaty benefits. The Commentaries to the OECD Model authorize a tax authority to deny benefits, under substance-over-form principles, to a nominee in one State deriving income from the other on behalf of a third-country resident. In addition, although the text of the OECD Model does not contain express anti-abuse provisions, the Commentaries to Article 1 contain an extensive discussion approving the use of such provisions in tax treaties in order to limit the ability of third state residents to obtain treaty benefits. The United States holds strongly to the view that tax treaties should include provisions that specifically prevent misuse of treaties by residents of third countries. Consequently, all recent U.S. income tax treaties contain comprehensive Limitation on Benefits provisions.

A treaty that provides treaty benefits to any resident of a Contracting State permits "treaty shopping": the use, by residents of third states, of legal entities established in a Contracting State with a principal purpose to obtain the benefits of a tax treaty between the United States and the other Contracting State. It is important to note that this definition of treaty shopping does not encompass every case in which a third state resident establishes an entity in a U.S. treaty partner, and that entity enjoys treaty benefits to which the third state resident would not itself be entitled. If the third country resident had substantial reasons for establishing the structure that were unrelated to obtaining treaty benefits, the structure would not fall within the definition of treaty shopping set forth above.

Of course, the fundamental problem presented by this approach is that it is based on the taxpayer's intent, which a tax administration is normally ill-equipped to identify. In order to avoid the necessity of making this subjective determination, Article 23 sets forth a series of mechanical tests. The assumption underlying each of these tests is that a taxpayer that satisfies the requirements of any of the tests probably has a real business purpose for the structure it has adopted, or has a sufficiently strong nexus to the other Contracting State (e.g., a resident individual) to warrant benefits even in the absence of a business connection, and that this business purpose or connection outweighs any purpose to obtain the benefits of the Convention.

For instance, the assumption underlying the active trade or business test under paragraph 3 is that a third country resident that establishes a "substantial" operation in Ireland and that derives income from a similar activity in the United States would not do so primarily to avail itself of the benefits of the Convention; it is presumed in such a case that the investor had a valid business purpose for investing in Ireland, and that the link between that trade or business and the U.S. activity that generates the treaty-benefitted income manifests a business purpose for placing the U.S. investments in the entity in Ireland. It is considered unlikely that the investor would incur the expense of establishing a substantial trade or business in Ireland simply to obtain the benefits of the Convention. A similar rationale underlies other tests in Article 23.

While mechanical tests provide useful surrogates for identifying actual intent, they cannot account for every case in which the taxpayer was not treaty shopping. Accordingly, Article 23 also includes a provision (paragraph 6) authorizing the competent authority of a Contracting State to grant benefits. While an analysis under paragraph 6 may well differ from that under one of the other tests of Article 23, its objective is the same: to identify investors whose residence in the other State can be justified by factors other than a purpose to derive treaty benefits.

Article 23 and the anti-abuse provisions of domestic law complement each other, as Article 23 effectively determines whether an entity has a sufficient nexus to the Contracting State to be treated as a resident for treaty purposes, while domestic anti-abuse provisions (e.g., business purpose, substance-over-form, step transaction or conduit principles) determine whether a particular transaction should be recast in accordance with its substance. Thus, internal law principles of the source State may be applied to identify the beneficial owner of an item of income, and Article 23 then will be applied to the beneficial owner to determine if that person is entitled to the benefits of the Convention with respect to such income.

*Structure of the Article*

Article 23 follows the form used in other recent U.S. income tax treaties. (See, e.g., the Convention between the United States of America and the Kingdom of the Netherlands for the Avoidance of Double Taxation and the Prevention of Fiscal Evasion with Respect to Taxes on Income.) The structure of the Article is as follows: Paragraph 1 states the general rule of the article that a resident is entitled to all the benefits otherwise accorded to residents only if such resident is a "qualified person" as defined in this Article. Paragraph 2 lists a series of six attributes of a resident, any one of which suffices to make such resident a "qualified person" and thus entitled to all the benefits of the Convention. Paragraph 3 sets forth the active trade or business test, under which a person not entitled to benefits under paragraph 2 may nonetheless be granted benefits with regard to certain types of income. Paragraph 4 provides for limited so-called "derivative benefits" for shipping and air transport income. Paragraph 5 provides a more general derivative benefits rule. Paragraph 6 provides that benefits also may be granted if the competent authority of the State from which benefits are claimed determines that it is appropriate to provide benefits in that case. Paragraph 7 limits treaty benefits in certain so-called "triangular" cases. Paragraph 8 defines the terms used specifically in this Article. Paragraph 9 authorizes the competent authorities to develop agreed applications of the provisions of this Article and to exchange information necessary to carry out the provisions of this Article.

*Paragraph 1*

Paragraph 1 provides that a resident of a Contracting State will be entitled to all the benefits of the Convention otherwise accorded to residents of a Contracting State only if the resident is a "qualified person" as defined in Article 23. The benefits otherwise accorded to residents under the Convention include all limitations on source-based taxation under Articles 6 through 22, the treaty-based relief from double taxation provided by Article 24 (Relief from Double Taxation), and the protection afforded to residents of a Contracting State under Article 25 (Non-Discrimination). Some provisions do not require that a person be a resident in order to enjoy the benefits of those provisions. These include paragraph 1 of Article 25 (Non-Discrimination), Article 26 (Mutual Agreement Procedure), and Article 28 (Diplomatic Agents and Consular Officers). Article 23 accordingly does not limit the availability of the benefits of these provisions.

*Paragraph 2*

Paragraph 2 has six subparagraphs, each of which describes a category of residents that constitute qualified persons and thus are entitled to all benefits of the Convention.

*Individuals -- Subparagraph 2(a)*

Subparagraph a) provides that individual residents of a Contracting State will be entitled to all treaty benefits. If such an individual receives income as a nominee on behalf of a third country resident, benefits may be denied under the respective articles of the Convention by the requirement that the beneficial owner of the income be a resident of a Contracting State.

*Qualified Governmental Entities -- Subparagraph 2(b)*

Subparagraph b) provides that qualified governmental entities, as defined in subparagraph 1(j) of Article 3 (Definitions), also will be entitled to all benefits of the Convention. As described in Article 3, in addition to federal, state and local governments, the term "qualified governmental entity" encompasses certain government-owned corporations and other entities, and certain pension trusts or funds that administer pension benefits described in Article 19 (Government Service).

*Ownership and Base Erosion -- Subparagraph 2(c)*

Subparagraph 2(c) provides a two-part test, the so-called ownership and base erosion test. This test applies to any form of legal entity that is a resident of a Contracting State. Both prongs or the test must be satisfied for the resident to be entitled to benefits under subparagraph 2(c).

The ownership prong of the test, under clause (i), requires that at least 50 percent of the beneficial interest in the person (or, in the case of a company, at least 50 percent of the aggregate vote and value of the company's shares) be owned by persons who are themselves entitled to benefits under the other tests of paragraph 2 (i.e., subparagraphs (a), (b), (d), (e), or (f)), or who are residents or citizens of the United States.

Although subparagraph 2(c) does not specify that only qualified persons described in other subparagraphs can satisfy the ownership test, this in fact is required by the rule regarding chains of ownership. Ownership by qualified persons may be indirect, but in cases of a chain of ownership, the ownership test must be satisfied by the last owners in the chain. In general, this requires that intermediate owners be disregarded and that ownership be traced to a person that is entitled to benefits without reference to its owners (such as a publicly traded company under subparagraph 2 (e)). Thus, owners that satisfy the test under subparagraph 2 (c) (i) include qualified persons described in subparagraphs 2(a), (b), (d), (e), and (f), because such persons are entitled to benefits without reference to their ownership (if any), or residents or citizens of the United States, because neither the United States nor Ireland is concerned about treaty-shopping through such persons. Ownership traced to any other person would not count towards satisfying the subparagraph 2(c)(i) ownership threshold.

Trusts may be entitled to benefits under this provision if they are treated as residents under Article 4 (Residence) and they otherwise satisfy the requirements of this subparagraph. For purposes of this subparagraph, the beneficial interests in a trust will be considered to be owned by its beneficiaries in proportion to each beneficiary's actuarial interest in the trust. The interest of a remainder beneficiary will be equal to 100 percent less the aggregate percentages held by income beneficiaries. A beneficiary's interest in a trust will not be considered to be owned by a person entitled to benefits under the provisions of paragraph 2 if it is not possible to determine the beneficiary's actuarial interest. Consequently, if it is not possible to determine the actuarial interest of any beneficiaries in a trust, the ownership test under clause (i) cannot be satisfied, unless all beneficiaries are persons entitled to benefits under the other subparagraphs of paragraph 2 or are residents or citizens of the United States.

The base erosion prong of the test under subparagraph 2(c) requires that amounts paid or accrued by a person during a taxable year, and deductible for tax purposes in that person's State of residence, to persons not entitled to benefits under paragraph 2 and not residents or citizens of the United States not constitute more than 50 percent of the person's gross income for that taxable year. To the extent they are deductible from the taxable base, trust distributions would be considered deductible payments. Depreciation and amortization deductions, which do not represent payments or accruals to other persons, are disregarded for this purpose. Deductible payments do not include arm's length payments in the ordinary course of business for services or tangible property or with respect to financial obligations to banks that are residents of either Contracting State or that have a permanent establishment in either Contracting State to which the payment is attributable. The exclusion of payments to banks is in recognition of the fact that a significant portion of the domestic banking market in Ireland has been accounted for by subsidiaries or branches of foreign banks. The U.S. Model also excludes from deductible payments those payments made to, and attributable to, a permanent establishment in a Contracting State.

The term "gross income" is not defined in this Convention. Thus, in accordance with paragraph 2 of Article 3 (General Definitions), in determining whether a person deriving income from United States sources is entitled to the benefits of the Convention, the United States will ascribe the meaning to the term that it has in the United States. In such cases, "gross income" will be defined as gross receipts less cost of goods sold. Subparagraph 8(a) allows the taxpayer to use an averaging rule, by providing that "gross income" for purposes of paragraph 2(c) means gross income for the preceding taxable year or the average of the annual amounts of gross income for the four taxable years preceding the current taxable year, whichever is greater.

*Publicly Traded Persons -- Subparagraph 2(d)*

Subparagraph d) applies to two categories of legal entities that may not be companies under the laws of one of the Contracting States: publicly traded entities and entities owned either by publicly traded companies or by publicly traded entities that are not individuals or companies. Clause i) of subparagraph 2(d) provides that a person other than an individual or a company will be entitled to all the benefits of the Convention if the principal class of "units" in that person is listed on a "recognized stock exchange" located in either State and is substantially and regularly traded. The term "units" is defined in subparagraph 8(c). The term "recognized stock exchange" is defined in subparagraph 8(b).

Subparagraph d) applies generally to trusts the shares of ownership in which are publicly traded and to trusts that are owned by publicly traded entities. From the U.S. perspective, the provision relating to publicly traded trusts is redundant, since the United States would generally consider such trusts to be corporations that are covered by the parallel provision under subparagraph 2(e).

The term "principal class of units" is not defined in the Convention. It is understood that it will be interpreted in accordance with the definition of "principal class of shares" in subparagraph 8(d).

The meaning of the term "substantially and regularly traded" in respect of the units in a class of units is defined in paragraph 9 of the Protocol to this Convention. The substantial and regular trading requirement can be met by trading on any recognized stock exchange. Trading on one or more recognized stock exchanges may be aggregated for purposes of this requirement. Thus, a U.S. entity could satisfy the substantially and regularly traded requirement through trading, in whole or in part, on a recognized stock exchange located in Ireland. Authorized but unissued units are not considered for purposes of this test.

Clause (ii) of subparagraph 2(d) provides a test under which certain entities are entitled to the benefits of the Convention if the direct or indirect owners of at least 50 percent of the beneficial interests in the entity are entities that satisfy the publicly traded test of subparagraph 2(d)(i) or 2(e)(i). Thus, for example, an Irish resident trust, all the shares of ownership in which are owned by a second Irish resident trust, would qualify for benefits under the Convention if the principal class of units of the second Irish trust were listed on the Irish Stock Exchange and substantially and regularly traded on the London stock exchange. However, the first Irish trust would not qualify for benefits under subparagraph 2(d)(ii) if the publicly traded second trust were a resident of the United Kingdom, not of the United States or Ireland. The requirement that the trust described in clause 2(d)(ii) be owned by a resident of one of the Contracting States is confirmed in paragraph 4 of the diplomatic notes.

*Publicly Traded Companies -- Subparagraph 2(e)*

Subparagraph e) applies to two categories of companies: publicly traded companies and subsidiaries of publicly traded companies. Clause i) of subparagraph 2(e) provides that a company will be entitled to all the benefits of the Convention if the principal class of its shares is substantially and regularly traded on one or more recognized stock exchanges. The term "recognized stock exchange" is defined in subparagraph 8(b) as (i) the NASDAQ System owned by the National Association of Securities Dealers, and any stock exchange registered with the Securities and Exchange Commission as a national securities exchange for purposes of the Securities Exchange Act of 1934; (ii) the Irish Stock Exchange and the stock exchanges of Amsterdam, Brussels, Frankfurt, Hamburg, London, Madrid, Milan, Paris, Stockholm, Sydney, Tokyo, Vienna and Zurich; and (iii) any other stock exchange agreed upon by the competent authorities of the Contracting States.

The term "principal class of shares" is defined in subparagraph 8(d). If a company has only one class of shares, it is only necessary to consider whether the shares of that class are substantially and regularly traded on a recognized stock exchange. If the company has more than one class of shares, it is necessary as an initial matter to determine whether one of the classes accounts for more than half of the voting power and value of the company. If so, then only those shares are considered for purposes of the substantial and regular trading requirement. If no single class of shares accounts for more than half of the company's voting power and value, it is necessary to identify a group of two or more classes of the company's shares that account for more than half of the company's voting power and value, and then to determine whether each class of shares in this group satisfies the regular trading requirement. Although in a particular case involving a company with several classes of shares it is conceivable that more than one group of classes could be identified that account for more than 50% of the shares, it is only necessary for one such group to satisfy the requirements of this subparagraph in order for the company to be entitled to benefits. Benefits would not be denied to the company even if a second, non-qualifying, group of shares with more than half of the company's voting power and value could be identified.

The principal class of shares must always include any disproportionate class of shares, as defined in subparagraph 8(d)(ii). A disproportionate class of shares means a class of shares in a company resident in one of the States that entitles the shareholder to a disproportionately higher share in the earnings generated in the other State by particular assets or activities of the company.

Such participation may take any form, including (but not limited to) dividends and redemption payments. A disproportionate class of shares would include so-called alphabet stock that entitles the holder to earnings in the State produced by a particular division of the company. The following examples illustrate the application of this paragraph.

Example 1. EIRECo is a corporation resident in Ireland. EIRECo has two classes of shares: Common and Preferred. The Common shares are listed on the Irish Stock Exchange and are substantially and regularly traded. The Preferred shares have no voting rights and are entitled to receive dividends equal in amount to interest payments that EIRECo receives from unrelated borrowers in the United States. The Common shares account for more than 50 percent of the value of EIRECo and for 100 percent of the voting power. Because the owner of the Preferred shares is entitled to receive payments corresponding to the U.S. source interest income earned by EIRECo, the Preferred shares are considered to be a disproportionate class of shares. Pursuant to subparagraph 8(d), the principal class of shares of EIRECo includes the Common and Preferred shares.

Example 2. EIRECo is a corporation resident in Ireland. EIRECo has two classes of shares: Common and Preferred. The Common shares are listed on the Irish Stock Exchange and are substantially and regularly traded. The Preferred shares have no voting rights and are entitled to receive dividends equal in amount to the income earned by EIRECo from selling widgets in Ireland. Because the Preferred shares do not entitle the owner to receive dividends or other payments corresponding to U.S.-source income received by EIRECo, the Preferred shares are not considered a disproportionate class of shares for purposes of subparagraph 8(d).

Paragraph 9 of the Protocol provides that a class of shares will be considered to be "substantially and regularly traded" on one or more recognized stock exchanges if trades in such class are effected on one or more such exchanges in other than de minimis quantities during every quarter of the taxable year for which benefits of the Convention are claimed and the aggregate number of shares of that class traded on such exchanges during the previous year is at least 6 percent of the average number of shares or units outstanding in that class during such previous year. The aggregate trading requirement is deemed to be met in the first year that a company is listed on a recognized stock exchange. In addition, Subparagraph 9(a)(ii) of the Protocol provides that an Irish Building Society will be deemed to satisfy the test under subparagraph 2(e) and hence is entitled to the benefits of the Convention.

The substantial and regular trading requirement can be met by trading on any recognized stock exchange. Trading on one or more recognized stock exchanges may be aggregated for purposes of this requirement. Thus, a U.S. company could satisfy the substantially and regularly traded requirement through trading, in whole or in part, on a recognized stock exchange located in Ireland or certain third countries. Authorized but unissued shares are not considered for purposes of this test.

Clause (ii) of subparagraph 2(e) provides a test under which a company resident in a Contracting State is entitled to the benefits of the Convention if the direct and indirect owners of at least 50 percent of the aggregate vote and value of the company's shares are publicly traded companies described in subparagraph 2(e)(i), qualified governmental entities, or companies more than 50 percent of the aggregate vote and value of which is owned by qualified governmental entities. Thus, for example, an Irish resident company, all the shares of ownership in which are owned by another Irish resident company, would qualify for benefits under the Convention if the principal class of shares of the Irish parent company were listed on the Irish Stock Exchange and substantially and regularly traded on the London stock exchange. However, the Irish company would not qualify for benefits under subparagraph 2(e)(ii) if the publicly traded parent company were a resident of the United Kingdom, not of the United States or Ireland. The requirement that the company described in clause 2(e)(ii) be owned by a resident of one of the Contracting States is confirmed in paragraph 4 of the diplomatic notes.

*Tax Exempt Organizations -- Subparagraph 2(f)*

Subparagraph 2(f) provides that the tax exempt organizations described in subparagraph 1(c) of Article 4 (Residence) will be qualified persons if more than half of the beneficiaries, members or participants of the organization are themselves entitled to treaty benefits under paragraph 2. Entities that may qualify under this subparagraph are those entities that generally are exempt from tax in their State of residence and that are organized and operated exclusively to administer and provide retirement and employee benefits or to fulfill religious, educational, scientific and other charitable purposes. For purposes of this provision, the term "beneficiaries" should be understood to refer to the persons receiving benefits from the organization.

The provisions of paragraph 2 are intended to be self executing. Unlike the provisions of paragraph 6, discussed below, claiming benefits under paragraph 2 does not require advance competent authority ruling or approval. The tax authorities may, of course, on review, determine that the taxpayer has improperly interpreted the paragraph and is not entitled to the benefits claimed.

*Paragraph 3*

Paragraph 3 sets forth a test under which a resident of a Contracting State that is not generally entitled to benefits of the Convention under paragraph 2 may receive treaty benefits with respect to certain items of income that are connected to an active trade or business conducted in its State of residence.

Subparagraph 3(a) sets forth a three-pronged test that must be satisfied in order for a resident of a Contracting State to be entitled to the benefits of the Convention with respect to a particular item of income. First, the resident must be engaged in the active conduct of a trade of business in its State of residence. Second, the income derived from the other State must be derived in connection with, or be incidental to, that trade or business. Third, if the resident has an ownership interest in the activity in the other State that generated the income, then the trade or business conducted by the resident in its State of residence must be substantial in relation to the activity in the other State that generated the item of income.

These determinations are made separately for each item of income derived from the other State. It therefore is possible that a person would be entitled to the benefits of the Convention with respect to one item of income but not with respect to another. If a resident of a Contracting State is entitled to treaty benefits with respect to a particular item of income under paragraph 3, the resident is entitled to all benefits of the Convention insofar as they affect the taxation of that item of income in the other State. Set forth below is a discussion of each of the three prongs of the test under paragraph 3.

*Trade or Business -- Subparagraph 3(a)(i)*

The term "trade or business" is not defined in the Convention. Pursuant to paragraph 2 of Article 3 (General Definitions), when determining whether a resident of the other State is entitled to the benefits of the Convention under paragraph 3 with respect to income derived from U.S. sources, the United States will ascribe to this term the meaning that it has under the law of the United States. Accordingly, the United States competent authority will refer to the regulations issued under section 367(a) for the definition of the term "trade or business." These regulations are consistent with the requirement under subparagraph 9(b)(i) of the Protocol, which states that this determination will be based on all the relevant facts and circumstances. In general, a trade or business will be considered to be a specific unified group of activities that constitute or could constitute an independent economic enterprise carried on for profit. Furthermore, a corporation generally will be considered to carry on a trade or business only if the officers and employees of the corporation conduct substantial managerial and operational activities. See, Code section 367(a)(3) and the regulations thereunder.

Notwithstanding this general definition of trade or business, subparagraph 3(a)(i) also provides that the business of making or managing investments, when part of banking or insurance activities conducted by a bank or insurance company acting in the ordinary course of its business, will be considered to be a trade or business. Conversely, such activities conducted by a person other than a bank or insurance company will not be considered to be the conduct of an active trade or business, nor would they be considered to be the conduct of an active trade or business if conducted by a banking or insurance company but not as part of the company's ordinary banking or insurance business. Subparagraphs 9(b)(i)(A) and (B) of the Protocol provide that a bank will be considered to be engaged in the active conduct of a banking business if it regularly accepts deposits from the public or makes loans to the public, and an insurance company will be considered to be engaged in the active conduct of an insurance business if its gross income consists primarily of insurance or reinsurance premiums and the investment income attributable to such premiums. Banks that, at the time of the signature of the Convention, were licensed by the banking authorities of a Contracting State to engage in a banking business are deemed to satisfy the active conduct requirement.

Because a headquarters operation is in the business of managing investments, a company that functions solely as a headquarters company will not be considered to be engaged in an active trade or business for purposes of paragraph 3.

Subparagraph 9(b)(ii) of the Protocol to the Convention provides that in determining whether a person is engaged in the active conduct of a trade or business in a Contracting State, activities conducted by a partnership in which that person is a partner and activities conducted by persons "connected" to such person will be deemed to be conducted by such person. Persons are deemed to be connected to each other if one owns at least 50 percent of the other or at least 50 percent of each is owned by another person. In addition, persons are connected if one controls the other or they are under common control.

*Derived in Connection With Requirement - Subparagraphs 3(a)(ii) and (b)(i)*

Subparagraph 3(b)(i) provides that income is derived in connection with a trade or business if the income-producing activity in the other State is a line of business that forms a part of or is complementary to the trade or business conducted in the State of residence by the income recipient. Although no definition of the terms "forms a part of" or "complementary" is set forth in the Convention, it is intended that a business activity generally will be considered to "form a part of" a business activity conducted in the other State if the two activities involve the design, manufacture or sale of the same products or type of products, or the provision of similar services. In order for two activities to be considered to be "complementary," the activities need not relate to the same types of products or services, but they should be part of the same overall industry and be related in the sense that the success or failure of one activity will tend to result in success or failure for the other. In cases in which more than one trade or business is conducted in the other State and only one of the trades or businesses forms a part of or is complementary to a trade or business conducted in the State of residence, it is necessary to identify the trade or business to which an item of income is attributable. Royalties generally will be considered to be derived in connection with the trade or business to which the underlying intangible property is attributable. Dividends will be deemed to be derived first out of earnings and profits of the treaty-benefitted trade or business, and then out of other earnings and profits. Interest income may be allocated under any reasonable method consistently applied. A method that conforms to U.S. principles for expense allocation will be considered a reasonable method. The following examples illustrate the application of subparagraph 3(b)(i).

Example 1. EIRECo is a corporation resident in Ireland. EIRECo is engaged in an active manufacturing business in Ireland. EIRECo owns 100 percent of the shares of USCo, a corporation resident in the United States. USCo distributes EIRECo products in the United States. Since the business activities conducted by the two corporations involve the same products, USCo's distribution business is considered to form a part of EIRECo's manufacturing business within the meaning of subparagraph 3(b)(i).

Example 2. The facts are the same as in Example 1, except that EIRECo does not manufacture. Rather, EIRECo operates a large research and development facility in Ireland that licenses intellectual property to affiliates worldwide, including USCo. USCo and other EIRECo affiliates then manufacture and market the EIRECo-designed products in their respective markets. Since the activities conducted by USCo and EIRECo involve the same product lines, these activities are considered to form a part of the same trade or business.

Example 3. Americair is a corporation resident in the United States that operates an international airline. FSub is a wholly owned subsidiary of Americair resident in Ireland. FSub operates a chain of hotels in Ireland that are located near airports served by Americair flights. Americair frequently sells tour packages that include air travel to Ireland and lodging at FSub hotels. Although both companies are engaged in the active conduct of a trade or business, the businesses of operating a chain of hotels and operating an airline are distinct trades or businesses. Therefore FSub's business does not form a part of Americair's business. However, FSub's business is considered to be complementary to Americair's business because they are part of the same overall industry (travel) and the links between their operations tend to make them interdependent.

Example 4. The facts are the same as in Example 3, except that FSub owns an office building in Ireland instead of a hotel chain. No part of Americair's business is conducted through the office building. FSub's business is not considered to form a part of or to be complementary to Americair's business. They are engaged in distinct trades or businesses in separate industries, and there is no economic dependence between the two operations.

Example 5. USFlower is a corporation resident in the United States. USFlower produces and sells flowers in the United States and other countries. USFlower owns all the shares of ForHolding, a corporation resident in Ireland. ForHolding is a holding company that is not engaged in a trade or business. ForHolding owns all the shares of three corporations that are resident in Ireland: ForFlower, ForLawn, and ForFish. ForFlower distributes USFlower flowers under the USFlower trademark in Ireland. ForLawn markets a line of lawn care products in Ireland under the USFlower trademark. In addition to being sold under the same trademark, ForLawn and ForFlower products are sold in the same stores and sales of each company's products tend to generate increased sales of the other's products. ForFish imports fish from the United States and distributes it to fish wholesalers in Ireland. For purposes of paragraph 3, the business of ForFlower forms a part of the business of USFlower, the business of ForLawn is complementary to the business of USFlower, and the business of ForFish is neither part of nor complementary to that of USFlower.

Finally, subparagraph 3(a)(ii) provides that a resident in one of the States also will be entitled to the benefits of the Convention with respect to income derived from the other State if the income is "incidental" to the trade or business conducted in the recipient's State of residence. Income derived from a State will be considered incidental to a trade or business conducted in the other State if the production of such income facilitates the conduct of the trade or business in the other State. An example of incidental income is the temporary investment of working capital derived from a trade or business.

*Substantiality -- Subparagraphs 3(a)(ii) and (b)(ii)*

As indicated above, subparagraph 3(a)(ii) provides that income that a resident of a State derives from the other State will be entitled to the benefits of the Convention under paragraph 3 only if the income is derived in connection with a trade or business conducted in the recipient's State of residence and, where such resident has an ownership interest in the income-producing activity in the other State, that trade or business is "substantial" in relation to the income-producing activity in the other State. Subparagraph 3(b)(ii) provides that whether the trade or business of the income recipient is substantial will be determined based on all the facts and circumstances. These circumstances generally would include the relative scale of the activities conducted in the two States and the relative contributions made to the conduct of the trade or businesses in the two States.

In addition to this subjective rule, subparagraph 3(b)(ii) provides a safe harbor under which the trade or business of the income recipient may be deemed to be substantial based on three ratios that compare the size of the recipient's activities to those conducted in the other State. The three ratios compare: (i) the value of the assets in the recipient's State to the assets used in the other State; (ii) the gross income derived in the recipient's State to the gross income derived in the other State; and (iii) the payroll expense in the recipient's State to the payroll expense in the other State. The average of the three ratios with respect to the preceding taxable year must exceed 10 percent, and each individual ratio must exceed 7.5 percent. If any individual ratio does not exceed 7.5 percent for the preceding taxable year, the average of the three preceding taxable years may be used instead. Thus, if the taxable year is 1998, the preceding year is 1997. If one of the ratios for 1997 is not greater than 7.5 percent, the average ratio for 1995, 1996, and 1997 with respect to that item may be used.

The term "value" also is not defined in the Convention. Therefore, this term also will be defined under U.S. law for purposes of determining whether a person deriving income from United States sources is entitled to the benefits of the Convention. In such cases, "value" generally will be defined using the method used by the taxpayer in keeping its books for purposes of financial reporting in its country of residence. See, Treas. Reg. §1.884-5(e)(3)(ii)(A).

Only items actually located or incurred in the two Contracting States are included in the computation of the ratios. If the person from whom the income in the other State is derived is not wholly owned (directly or indirectly) by the recipient then the items included in the computation with respect to such person must be reduced by a percentage equal to the percentage ownership held by persons other than the recipient. For instance, if an Irish corporation derives income from a U.S. corporation in which it holds 80 percent of the shares, for purposes of subparagraph 3(b)(ii) only 80 percent of the assets, payroll and gross income of the U.S. company would be taken into account.

If the recipient has no ownership interest in the person from whom the income is derived, then pursuant to subparagraph 3(a)(ii) the substantiality test does not apply. Of course, the other two prongs of the test under paragraph 3 would have to be satisfied in order for the recipient of the item of income to receive treaty benefits with respect to that income. For example, assume that a resident of a Ireland is in the business of banking in Ireland. The bank loans money to unrelated residents of the United States. The bank would not be subject to the substantiality requirement of subparagraph 3(a)(ii) with respect to interest paid on the loans because it has no ownership interest in the payors.

The provisions of paragraph 3 are intended to be self executing. Unlike the provisions of paragraph 6, discussed below, claiming benefits under paragraph 3 does not require advance competent authority ruling or approval. The tax authorities may, of course, on review, determine that the taxpayer has improperly interpreted the paragraph and is not entitled to the benefits claimed.

*Paragraph 4*

Paragraph 4 provides that a resident of one of the States that derives income from the other State described in Article 8 (Shipping and Air Transport) and that is not entitled to the benefits of the Convention under paragraphs 1 through 3, shall nonetheless be entitled to the benefits of the Convention with respect to income described in Article 8 if it meets one of two tests. These tests in substance duplicate the rules set forth under Code section 883 and therefore afford little additional benefit beyond those provided by the Code. These tests are described below.

First, a resident of one of the States will be entitled to the benefits of the Convention with respect to income described in Article 8 if at least 50 percent of the beneficial interest in the person (in the case of a company, at least 50 percent of the aggregate vote and value of the stock of the company) is owned, directly or indirectly, by qualified persons or citizens of the United States or individuals who are residents of a third state that grants by law, common agreement, or convention an exemption under similar terms for profits as mentioned in Article 8 to citizens and corporations of the other State. This provision is analogous to the relief provided under Code section 883(c)(1).

Alternatively, a resident of one of the States will be entitled to the benefits of the Convention with respect to income described in Article 8 if at least 50 percent of the beneficial of the person (in the case of a company, at least 50 percent of the aggregate vote and value of the stock of the company) is owned directly or indirectly by a company or combination of companies the principal class of shares in which is substantially and regularly traded on an established securities market in a third state, provided that the third state grants by law, common agreement or convention an exemption under similar terms for profits as mentioned in Article 8 to citizens and corporations of the other State. This provision is analogous to the relief provided under Code section 883(c)(3). The term "substantially and regularly traded on an established securities market" is not defined in the Convention. In determining whether a resident of Ireland is entitled to the benefits of the Convention under this paragraph, the United States will refer to the principles of Code section 883(c)(3)(A) for guidance as to the definition of this term.

The provisions of paragraph 4 are intended to be self executing. Unlike the provisions of paragraph 6, discussed below, claiming benefits under paragraph 4 does not require advance competent authority ruling or approval. The tax authorities may, of course, on review, determine that the taxpayer has improperly interpreted the paragraph and is not entitled to the benefits claimed.

*Paragraph 5*

Paragraph 5 sets forth a limited derivative benefits test that applies to all treaty benefits. In general, a derivative benefits test entitles the resident of a state to treaty benefits if the beneficial owner of the resident would have been entitled to the same benefit had the income in question flowed directly to that owner. Paragraph 5 provides a derivative benefits test under which a company that is a resident of a Contracting State may be entitled to some or all of the benefits of the Convention. In order to be entitled to all the benefits of the Convention under this paragraph, the company must meet an ownership test, a base reduction test, and a derivative benefits test. These tests are described below.

Subparagraph 5(a)(i) sets forth the ownership test. Under this test, at least 95 percent of the aggregate vote and value of the company's shares must be owned by any combination of seven or fewer persons that are entitled to all of the benefits of the Convention under paragraph 2 or are residents of member states of the European Union or of parties to NAFTA. Ownership may be direct or indirect.

Pursuant to subparagraphs 8(e) and (f) of this Article, a person will be considered a resident of a member state of the European Union or of a party to NAFTA for purposes of this paragraph only if the person would be entitled to the benefits of the income tax treaty between its state of residence and the Contracting State from which treaty benefits are claimed. However, if that treaty does not contain a comprehensive limitation on benefits provision, then that person must be a person who would still have qualified for the benefits of that treaty under provisions analogous to the provisions of paragraph 2 of this Article had that treaty contained a limitation on benefits provision with those provisions.

Subparagraph 5(a)(ii) sets forth the base reduction test. This test is the same as the base reduction test in subparagraph 2(c)(ii), except that for purposes of this test amounts paid or accrued to persons that are residents of a member state of the European Union or of a party to NAFTA are excluded from deductible payments.

Notwithstanding subparagraph 5(a), subparagraph 5(b) sets forth an additional requirement that must be satisfied in order for a company that is a resident of a Contracting State to be entitled to the benefits of the Convention accorded under Articles 10 (Dividends), 11 (Interest) or 12 (Royalties). This provision requires a comparison of the rate of tax imposed on a particular payment under the Convention to the rate of tax that would be imposed under the income tax convention between the source state and any European Union member state or party to NAFTA whose residents account for some of the ownership interest described in subparagraph 5(a)(i). Benefits will be extended with respect to such a payment under this provision only if at least 95 percent of the company's shares are owned by persons resident in a European Union member state or a party to NAFTA for which the rate (or rates) of withholding tax provided in the income tax convention between the source state and such state is less than or equal to the rate or rates imposed under the Convention. This rate comparison is by definition satisfied for persons owning shares that are also qualified persons under paragraph 2 of this Article. If for a particular payment less than 95 percent of the ownership interest is accounted for by persons that satisfy the rate comparison, then paragraph 5 does not apply to that payment (although it may apply to other payments and would apply to items of income, profit or gain other than those referred to in subparagraph 5(b)).

The rates of tax to be compared under this paragraph are the rate of withholding tax that the source State would impose had the European Union or NAFTA resident directly received its proportionate share of the dividend, interest or royalty payment and the rate of withholding tax that the source State would have imposed had that person been a resident of the other State and the person's proportionate share of the dividend, interest or royalty payment had been paid directly to that person. For example, assume that a U.S. company pays a dividend to EIRECo, a company resident in Ireland. EIRECo has two equal shareholders, a corporation resident in the United Kingdom and an individual resident in the United Kingdom. Both are residents of a member state of the European Union within the meaning of paragraph 5. Each person's proportionate share of the dividend payment is 50 percent of the dividend. If the UK corporation had received this portion of the dividend directly, it would be subject to a withholding tax of 5 percent under the income tax treaty between the United States and the United Kingdom. If the individual had received his portion of the dividend directly, it would be subject to a withholding tax of 15 percent under the same treaty. These rates are the same rates that would have applied if the corporation and the individual had been residents of Ireland. Therefore, the test under subparagraph 5 (b) is satisfied with respect to this dividend payment.

The provisions of paragraph 5 are intended to be self executing. Unlike the provisions of paragraph 6, discussed below, claiming benefits under paragraph 5 does not require advance competent authority ruling or approval. The tax authorities may, of course, on review, determine that the taxpayer has improperly interpreted the paragraph and is not entitled to the benefits claimed.

*Paragraph 6*

Paragraph 6 provides that a resident of one of the States that is not otherwise entitled to the benefits of the Convention may be granted benefits under the Convention if the competent authority of the State from which benefits are claimed so determines. This discretionary provision is included in recognition of the fact that, with the increasing scope and diversity of international economic relations, there may be cases where significant participation by third country residents in an enterprise of a Contracting State is warranted by sound business practice or long-standing business structures and does not necessarily indicate a motive of attempting to derive unintended Convention benefits.

Paragraph 6 provides that the competent authority of a State will base a determination under this paragraph on whether the establishment, acquisition, or maintenance of the person seeking benefits under the Convention, or the conduct of such person's operations, has or had as one of its principal purposes the obtaining of benefits under the Convention. Thus, persons that establish operations in one of the States with the principal purpose of obtaining the benefits of the Convention ordinarily will not be granted relief under paragraph 6.

The competent authority may determine to grant all benefits of the Convention, or it may determine to grant only certain benefits. For instance, it may determine to grant benefits only with respect to a particular item of income in a manner similar to paragraph 3. Further, the competent authority may set time limits on the duration of any relief granted.

It is assumed that, for purposes of implementing paragraph 6, a taxpayer will not be required to wait until the tax authorities of one of the States have determined that benefits are denied before he will be permitted to seek a determination under this paragraph. In these circumstances, it is also expected that if the competent authority determines that benefits are to be allowed, they will be allowed retroactively to the time of entry into force of the relevant treaty provision or the establishment of the structure in question, whichever is later.

The competent authority of a Contracting State will consult with the competent authority of the other Contracting State before denying the benefits of the Convention under paragraph 6.

Finally, there may be cases in which a resident of a Contracting State may apply for discretionary relief to the competent authority of his State of residence. For instance, a resident of a State could apply to the competent authority of his State of residence in a case in which he had been denied a treaty-based credit under Article 24 on the grounds that he was not entitled to benefits of the article under Article 23.

*Paragraph 7*

Paragraph 7 addresses the so-called "triangular case" in which an Irish enterprise derives income from the United States and that income is attributable to a permanent establishment located in a third jurisdiction that imposes little or no income tax on those profits. This provision is necessary to prevent triangular case abuse since Ireland may in particular circumstances exempt from tax profits attributable to a permanent establishment of its residents located in certain countries, although it would tax the income, subject to a foreign tax credit, if the income were earned directly by the Irish entity.

The Contracting States agreed that it would be inappropriate to grant treaty benefits with respect to such income. Therefore, paragraph 7 generally denies any treaty benefit with respect to any item of income derived by an Irish resident enterprise and attributable to a permanent establishment in a third state if the combined tax in Ireland and the third state is less than 50 percent of the tax that normally would be imposed in Ireland if the income were earned there and were not attributable to the permanent establishment in the third state. Paragraph 7 further provides that any dividends, interest or royalties to which this paragraph applies shall be subject to tax at source under domestic law, but at a rate not exceeding 15 percent of the gross amount.

Paragraph 7 provides an exception that grants treaty benefits for income that is connected with or incidental to the active conduct of a trade or business carried on by the permanent establishment in the third state. The business of making or managing investments is not an active trade or business for this purpose unless the activities are banking or insurance activities carried on by a bank or insurance company.

*Paragraph 8*

Paragraph 8 defines key terms used in this Article, which are discussed above in connection with the relevant paragraphs.

*Paragraph 9*

Paragraph 9 provides additional authority to the competent authorities (in addition to that of Article 26 (Mutual Agreement Procedure)) to consult together to develop a common application of the provisions of this Article, including the publication of regulations or other public guidance. The competent authorities shall, in accordance with the provisions of Article 27 (Exchange of Information and Administrative Assistance) exchange such information as is necessary to carry out the provisions of this Article.

## Article 24 (Relief from Double Taxation)

This Article describes the manner in which each Contracting State undertakes to relieve double taxation. The United States uses the foreign tax credit method under its internal law, and by treaty. Ireland uses a foreign tax credit when provided by a treaty and in certain circumstances under its domestic law. In other cases, it provides for a deduction of the tax against the relevant income.

*Paragraph 1*

The United States agrees, in paragraph 1, to allow to its citizens and residents a credit against U.S. tax for income taxes paid or accrued to Ireland. This provision is based on the Treasury Department's review of Ireland's laws.

The credit under the Convention is allowed in accordance with the provisions and subject to the limitations of U.S. law, as that law may be amended over time, so long as the general principle of this Article, i.e., the allowance of a credit, is retained. Thus, although the Convention provides for a foreign tax credit, the terms of the credit are determined by the provisions, at the time a credit is given, of the U.S. statutory credit.

Subparagraph (b) provides for a deemed-paid credit, consistent with section 902 of the Code, to a U.S. corporation in respect of dividends received from a corporation resident in Ireland of which the U.S. corporation owns at least 10 percent of the voting stock. This credit is for the tax paid by the corporation of Ireland on the profits out of which the dividends are considered paid.

As indicated, the U.S. credit under the Convention is subject to the various limitations of U.S. law (see Code sections 901 - 908). For example, the credit against U.S. tax generally is limited to the amount of U.S. tax due with respect to net foreign source income within the relevant foreign tax credit limitation category (see Code section 904(a) and (d)), and the dollar amount of the credit is determined in accordance with U.S. currency translation rules (see, e.g., Code section 986). Similarly, U.S. law applies to determine carryover periods for excess credits and other inter-year adjustments. When the alternative minimum tax is due, the alternative minimum tax foreign tax credit generally is limited in accordance with U.S. law to 90 percent of alternative minimum tax liability. Furthermore, nothing in the Convention prevents the limitation of the U.S. credit from being applied on a per-country basis (should internal law be changed), an overall basis, or to particular categories of income (see, e.g., Code section 865(h)).

*Paragraph 2*

Under subparagraph 3(b) of Article 10 (Dividends), Ireland allows individual residents of the United States certain tax credits or refunds in respect of dividends paid by a corporation which is a resident of Ireland, subject to taxes withheld of 15 percent on the aggregate amounts received as dividends and tax credits. Paragraph 2 provides that the amounts withheld by Ireland pursuant to paragraph 3(b) shall be regarded as an income tax imposed on the recipient of the dividend. Thus, the U.S. foreign tax credit with respect to those amounts shall be computed in accordance with Code section 901.

*Paragraph 3*

Paragraph 3 provides special rules for the tax treatment in both States of certain types of income derived from U.S. sources by U.S. citizens who are resident in Ireland. Since U.S. citizens, regardless of residence, are subject to United States tax at ordinary progressive rates on their worldwide income, the U.S. tax on the U.S. source income of a U.S. citizen resident in Ireland may exceed the U.S. tax that may be imposed under the Convention on an item of U.S. source income derived by a resident of Ireland who is not a U.S. citizen.

Subparagraph (a) of paragraph 3 provides special credit rules for Ireland with respect to items of income that are either exempt from U.S. tax or subject to reduced rates of U.S. tax under the provisions of the Convention when received by residents of Ireland who are not U.S. citizens. The tax credit of Ireland allowed by paragraph 3(a) under these circumstances, to the extent consistent with the law of that State, need not exceed the U.S. tax that may be imposed under the provisions of the Convention, other than tax imposed solely by reason of the U.S. citizenship of the taxpayer under the provisions of the saving clause of paragraph 4 of Article 1 (General Scope). Thus, if a U.S. citizen resident in Ireland receives U.S. source portfolio dividends, the foreign tax credit granted by that other State would be limited to 15 percent of the dividend -- the U.S. tax that may be imposed under subparagraph 2(b) of Article 10 (Dividends) -- even if the shareholder is subject to U.S. net income tax because of his U.S. citizenship. With respect to royalty or interest income, Ireland would allow no foreign tax credit, because its residents are exempt from U.S. tax on these classes of income under the provisions of Articles 11 (Interest) and 12 (Royalties).

Paragraph 3(b) eliminates the potential for double taxation that can arise because subparagraph 3(a) provides that Ireland need not provide full relief for the U.S. tax imposed on its citizens resident in Ireland. The subparagraph provides that the United States will credit the income tax paid or accrued to Ireland, after the application of subparagraph 3(a). It further provides that in allowing the credit, the United States will not reduce its tax below the amount that is taken into account in Ireland in applying subparagraph 3(a). Since the income described in paragraph 3 is U.S. source income, special rules are required to resource some of the income to Ireland in order for the United States to be able to credit the other State's tax. This resourcing is provided for in subparagraph 3(c), which deems the items of income referred to in subparagraph 3(a) to be from foreign sources to the extent necessary to avoid double taxation under paragraph 3(b). The rules of paragraph 3(c) apply only for purposes of determining U.S. foreign tax credits with respect to taxes referred to in paragraphs 1(b) and 2 of Article 2 (Taxes Covered).

The following two examples illustrate the application of paragraph 3 in the case of a U.S. source portfolio dividend received by a U.S. citizen resident in Ireland. In both examples, the U.S. rate of tax on residents of the other State under paragraph 2(b) of Article 10 (Dividends) of the Convention is 15 percent. In both examples the U.S. income tax rate on the U.S. citizen is 36 percent. In example I, Ireland's income tax rate on its resident (the U.S. citizen) is 25 percent (below the U.S. rate), and in example II, Ireland's income tax rate on its resident is 40 percent (above the U.S. rate).

| | Example I | Example II |
|---|---|---|
| Paragraph 3(a) | | |
| U.S. dividend declared | $100.00 | $100.00 |
| Notional U.S. withholding tax per Article 10(2)(b) | 15.00 | 15.00 |
| Irish taxable income | 100.00 | 100.00 |

| | | |
|---|---|---|
| Irish tax before credit | 25.00 | 40.00 |
| Irish foreign tax credit | 15.00 | 15.00 |
| Net post-credit Irish tax | 10.00 | 25.00 |

|                                          | Example I  | Example II |
|------------------------------------------|-----------|-----------|
| Paragraphs 3(b) and (c)                  |           |           |
| U.S. pre-tax income                      | $100.00   | $100.00   |
| U.S. pre-credit citizenship tax          | 36.00     | 36.00     |
| Notional U.S. withholding tax            | 15.00     | 15.00     |
| U.S. tax available for credit            | 21.00     | 21.00     |
| Income resourced from U.S. to Ireland    | 27.77     | 58.33     |
| U.S. tax on resourced income             | 10.00     | 21.00     |
| U.S. credit for Irish tax                | 10.00     | 21.00     |
| Net post-credit U.S. tax                 | 11.00     | 0.00      |
| Total U.S. tax                           | 26.00     | 15.00     |

In both examples, in the application of paragraph 3(a), Ireland credits a 15 percent U.S. tax against its residence tax on the U.S. citizen. In example I the net Irish tax after foreign tax credit is $10.00; in the second example it is $25.00. In the application of paragraphs 3(b) and (c), from the U.S. tax due before credit of $36.00, the United States subtracts the amount of the U.S. source tax of $15.00, against which no U.S. foreign tax credit is to be allowed. This provision assures that the United States will collect the tax that it is due under the Convention as the source country. In both examples, the maximum amount of U.S. tax against which credit for Irish tax may be claimed is $21.00. Initially, all of the income in these examples was U.S. source. In order for a U.S. credit to be allowed for the full amount of the Irish tax, an appropriate amount of the income must be resourced. The amount that must be resourced depends on the amount of Irish tax for which the U.S. citizen is claiming a U.S. foreign tax credit. In example I, the Irish tax was $10.00. In order for this amount to be creditable against U.S. tax, $27.77 ($10 divided by .36) must be resourced as foreign source. When the Irish tax is credited against the U.S. tax on the resourced income, there is a net U.S. tax of $11.00 due after credit. In example II, Irish tax was $25 but, because the amount available for credit is reduced under subparagraph 3(c) by the amount of the U.S. source tax, only $21.00 is eligible for credit. Accordingly, the amount that must be resourced is limited to the amount necessary to ensure a foreign tax credit for $21 of Irish tax, or $58.33 ($21 divided by .36). Thus, even though Irish tax was $25.00 and the U.S. tax available for credit was $21.00, there is no excess credit available for carryover.

*Paragraph 4*

Ireland agrees, in paragraph 4, to allow a credit against Irish tax for United States taxes paid with respect to profits, income or chargeable gains from U.S. sources, to the extent the tax is imposed in accordance with the Convention. The credit under the Convention is allowed in accordance with the provisions and subject to the limitations of Irish law, as that law may be amended over time, so long as the general principle of this Article, i.e., the allowance of a credit, is retained. Thus, although the Convention provides for a foreign tax credit, the terms of the credit are determined by the provisions, at the time a credit is given, of the Irish statutory credit.

Subparagraph (b) provides for a deemed-paid credit to an Irish corporation in respect of dividends received from a corporation resident in the United States of which the Irish corporation owns at least 10 percent of the voting stock. This credit is for the tax paid by the corporation of Ireland on the profits out of which the dividends are considered paid.

*Paragraph 5*

Paragraph 5 provides that, for purposes of this Article, income which may be taxed in a Contracting State under the terms of this Convention will be considered to have its source in that State. However, domestic law source rules that apply for purposes of limiting the foreign tax credit will govern if they differ from the results under this paragraph. This permits the United States to apply the anti-abuse rules of Code section 904(g), for example.

*Paragraph 6*

Paragraph 6 is included in the Convention because Ireland continues to maintain a remittance system of taxation for individuals who are resident but not domiciled in Ireland. Such persons are subject to tax in Ireland on non-Irish source income only to the extent the income or chargeable gains are remitted to the Irish resident. Under paragraph 6, such persons are entitled to the benefits of the Convention in order to reduce or eliminate tax only to the extent that the relevant income is remitted or received. For example, if an Irish resident individual who is not domiciled in Ireland maintains a brokerage account in the United Kingdom into which is paid $100 in U.S.-source dividend income, the United States may impose withholding tax at the statutory rate of 30%. If the dividend income instead is paid into a brokerage account in Dublin, the Irish resident will be subject to tax in Ireland and the United States will reduce the withholding tax to 15%.

Domicile is a legal concept that is not necessarily related to residence. An individual receives a domicile of origin at birth. The individual may change that domicile by physically relocating with the intention of changing his domicile.

*Relation to other articles*

By virtue of the exceptions in subparagraph 5(a) of Article 1 this Article is not subject to the saving clause of paragraph 4 of Article 1 (General Scope). Thus, the United States will allow a credit to its citizens and residents in accordance with the Article, even if such credit were to provide a benefit not available under the Code.

## Article 25 (Non-discrimination)

This Article assures that nationals of a Contracting State, in the case of paragraph 1, and residents of a Contracting State, in the case of paragraphs 2 through 4, will not be subject, directly or indirectly, to discriminatory taxation in the other Contracting State. For this purpose, nondiscrimination means providing national treatment. Not all differences in tax treatment, either as between nationals of the two States, or between residents of the two States, are violations of this national treatment standard. Rather, the national treatment obligation of this Article applies only if the nationals or residents of the two States are comparably situated.

Each of the relevant paragraphs of the Article provides that two persons that are comparably situated must be treated similarly. Although the actual words differ from paragraph to paragraph (e.g., paragraph 1 refers to two nationals "in the same circumstances," paragraph 2 refers to two enterprises "carrying on the same activities" and paragraph 4 refers to two enterprises that are "similar"), the common underlying premise is that if the difference in treatment is directly related to a tax-relevant difference in the situations of the domestic and foreign persons being compared, that difference is not to be treated as discriminatory (e.g., if one person is taxable in a Contracting State on worldwide income and the other is not, or tax may be collectible from one person at a later stage, but not from the other, distinctions in treatment would be justified under paragraph 1). Other examples of such factors that can lead to non-discriminatory differences in treatment will be noted in the discussions of each paragraph.

The operative paragraphs of the Article also use different language to identify the kinds of differences in taxation treatment that will be considered discriminatory. For example, paragraphs 1 and 4 speak of "any taxation or any requirement connected therewith that is other or more burdensome," while paragraph 2 specifies that a tax "shall not be less favorably levied." Regardless of these differences in language, only differences in tax treatment that materially disadvantage the foreign person relative to the domestic person are properly the subject of the Article.

In most U.S. tax treaties, like the U.S. and OECD Models, this Article applies to taxes of every kind and description imposed by a Contracting State or a political subdivision or local authority thereof for purposes of providing nondiscrimination protection. This provision has not been included in the Convention because of restrictions in Irish law.

*Paragraph 1*

Paragraph 1 provides that a national of one Contracting State may not be subject to taxation or connected requirements in the other Contracting State that are other than or more burdensome than the taxes and connected requirements imposed upon a national of that other State in the same circumstances. This language is consistent with the OECD Model.

As noted above, whether or not the two persons are both taxable on worldwide income is a significant circumstance for this purpose. The 1992 revision of the OECD Model adds after the words "in the same circumstances, the phrase "in particular with respect to residence," reflecting the fact that under most countries' laws residents are taxable on worldwide income and nonresidents are not.

Because the relevant circumstances relate, among other things, to taxation on worldwide income, paragraph 1 does not obligate a Contracting State to apply the same taxing regime to a citizen of the other Contracting State who is not resident in the first-mentioned Contracting State and a citizen of that State who is not resident in that State. For example, United States citizens who are not residents of the United States but who are, nevertheless, subject to U.S. tax on their worldwide income are not in the same circumstances with respect to U.S. taxation as citizens of Ireland who are not United States residents. Thus, for example, Article 25 would not entitle a national of Ireland resident in a third country to taxation at graduated rates of U.S. source dividends or other investment income that applies to a U.S. citizen resident in the same third country. The underlying concept is essentially the same as that underlying the OECD Model provision and similar provisions in the U.S. Model.

A national of a Contracting State is afforded protection under this paragraph even if the national is not a resident of either Contracting State. Thus, a U.S. citizen who is resident in a third country is entitled, under this paragraph, to the same treatment in Ireland as a national of Ireland who is in similar circumstances (i.e., presumably one who is resident in a third State). The term "national" in relation to a Contracting State is defined in subparagraph 1(i) of Article 3 (General Definitions).

Like the prior Convention and the U.S. and OECD Models, the scope of paragraph 1 extends beyond individuals to cover juridical persons that are nationals of a Contracting State. The inclusion of juridical persons in paragraph 1, however, generally may add little as a practical matter to the scope of the Article as a whole. A corporation that is a national of Ireland and is doing business in the United States is already protected, vis-a-vis a U.S. corporation, by paragraph 2. If a foreign corporation is not doing business in the United States it is, in relevant respect, in different circumstances from a U.S. corporation, and is, therefore, not entitled to national treatment in the United States. With respect to U.S. nationals claiming nondiscrimination protection from the treaty partner, U.S. corporations that are "nationals" of the United States are also U.S. residents and are, therefore, protected by paragraphs 2 and 4 in any event.

*Paragraph 2*

Paragraph 2 of the Article, like the comparable paragraphs in the U.S. and OECD Models, provides that a Contracting State may not tax a permanent establishment or fixed base of an enterprise of the other Contracting State less favorably than an enterprise of that first-mentioned State that is carrying on the same activities. This provision, however, does not obligate a Contracting State to grant to a resident of the other Contracting State any tax allowances, reliefs, etc., that it grants to its own residents on account of their civil status or family responsibilities. Thus, if a sole proprietor who is a resident of Ireland has a permanent establishment in the United States, in assessing income tax on the profits attributable to the permanent establishment, the United States is not obligated to allow to the resident of Ireland the personal allowances for himself and his family that he would be permitted to take if the permanent establishment were a sole proprietorship owned and operated by a U.S. resident, despite the fact that the individual income tax rates would apply.

The fact that a U.S. permanent establishment of an enterprise of Ireland is subject to U.S. tax only on income that is attributable to the permanent establishment, while a U.S. corporation engaged in the same activities is taxable on its worldwide income is not, in itself, a sufficient difference to deny national treatment to the permanent establishment. There are cases, however, where the two enterprises would not be similarly situated and differences in treatment may be warranted. For instance, it would not be a violation of the nondiscrimination protection of paragraph 2 to require the foreign enterprise to provide information in a reasonable manner that may be different from the information requirements imposed on a resident enterprise, because information may not be as readily available to the Internal Revenue Service from a foreign as from a domestic enterprise. Similarly, it would not be a violation of paragraph 2 to impose penalties on persons who fail to comply with such a requirement (see, e.g., sections 874(a) and 882(c)(2)). Further, a determination that income and expenses have been attributed or allocated to a permanent establishment in conformity with the principles of Article 7 (Business Profits) implies that the attribution or allocation was not discriminatory.

Section 1446 of the Code imposes on any partnership with income that is effectively connected with a U.S. trade or business the obligation to withhold tax on amounts allocable to a foreign partner. In the context of the Convention, this obligation applies with respect to a share of the partnership income of a partner resident in Ireland, and attributable to a U.S. permanent establishment. There is no similar obligation with respect to the distributive shares of U.S. resident partners. It is understood, however, that this distinction is not a form of discrimination within the meaning of paragraph 2 of the Article. No distinction is made between U.S. and non-U.S. partnerships, since the law requires that partnerships of both U.S. and non-U.S. domicile withhold tax in respect of the partnership shares of non-U.S. partners. Furthermore, in distinguishing between U.S. and non-U.S. partners, the requirement to withhold on the non-U.S. but not the U.S. partner's share is not discriminatory taxation, but, like other withholding on nonresident aliens, is merely a reasonable method for the collection of tax from persons who are not continually present in the United States, and as to whom it otherwise may be difficult for the United States to enforce its tax jurisdiction. If tax has been over-withheld, the partner can, as in other cases of over-withholding, file for a refund. (The relationship between paragraph 2 and the imposition of the branch tax is dealt with below in the discussion of paragraph 5.)

Paragraph 2, like the U.S. Model, goes beyond the comparable paragraphs in the OECD Model in that it obligates the host State to provide national treatment not only to permanent establishments of an enterprise of the other Contracting State, but also to other residents of that State that are taxable in the host State on a net basis because they derive income from independent personal services performed in the host State that is attributable to a fixed base in that State. Thus, an individual resident of Ireland who performs independent personal services in the U.S., and who is subject to U.S. income tax on the income from those services that is attributable to a fixed base in the United States, is entitled to no less favorable tax treatment in the United

States than a U.S. resident engaged in the same kinds of activities.  With such a rule in a treaty, the host State cannot tax its own residents on a net basis, but disallow deductions (other than personal allowances, etc.) with respect to the income attributable to the fixed base.  Similarly, in accordance with paragraph 5 of Article 6 (Income from Real Property (Immovable Property)), the situs State would be required to allow deductions to a resident of the other State with respect to income derived from real property located in the situs State to the same extent that deductions are allowed to residents of the situs State with respect to income derived from real property located in the situs State.

*Paragraph 3*

Paragraph 3 prohibits discrimination in the allowance of deductions.  When an enterprise of a Contracting State pays interest, royalties or other disbursements to a resident of the other Contracting State, the first-mentioned Contracting State must allow a deduction for those payments in computing the taxable profits of the enterprise as if the payment had been made under the same conditions to a resident of the first-mentioned Contracting State.  An exception to this rule is provided for cases where the provisions of paragraph 1 of Article 9 (Associated Enterprises), paragraph 5 of Article 11 (Interest) or paragraph 4 of Article 12 (Royalties) apply, because all of these provisions permit the denial of deductions in certain circumstances in respect of transactions between related persons.  This exception would include the denial or deferral of certain interest deductions under Code section 163(j).

The term "other disbursements" is understood to include a reasonable allocation of executive and general administrative expenses, research and development expenses and other expenses incurred for the benefit of a group of related persons that includes the person incurring the expense.

Because, as noted above, Article 25 applies only to covered taxes, Paragraph 3 differs from the U.S. and OECD Models in that it omits rules regarding the deductibility of debts for purposes of computing the capital tax of an enterprise.

*Paragraph 4*

Paragraph 4 requires that a Contracting State not impose more burdensome taxation or connected requirements on an enterprise of that State that is wholly or partly owned or controlled, directly or indirectly, by one or more residents of the other Contracting State, than the taxation or connected requirements that it imposes on other similar enterprises of that first-mentioned Contracting State.  For this purpose it is understood that "similar" refers to similar activities or ownership of the enterprise.

The Tax Reform Act of 1986 changed the rules for taxing corporations on certain distributions they make in liquidation.  Prior to 1986, corporations were not taxed on distributions of appreciated property in complete liquidation, although nonliquidating distributions of the same property, with several exceptions, resulted in corporate-level tax. In part to eliminate this disparity, the law now generally taxes corporations on the liquidating distribution of appreciated property. The Code provides an exception in the case of distributions by 80 percent or more controlled subsidiaries to their parent corporations, on the theory that the built-in gain in the asset will be recognized when the parent sells or distributes the asset. This exception does not apply to distributions to parent corporations that are tax-exempt organizations or, except to the extent provided in regulations, foreign corporations. The policy of the legislation is to collect one corporate-level tax on the liquidating distribution of appreciated property. If, and only if, that tax can be collected on a subsequent sale or distribution does the legislation defer the tax. It is understood that the inapplicability of the exception to the tax on distributions to foreign parent corporations under section 367(e)(2) does not conflict with paragraph 4 of the Article. While a liquidating distribution to a U.S. parent will not be taxed, and, except to the extent provided in regulations, a liquidating distribution to a foreign parent will, paragraph 4 merely prohibits discrimination among corporate taxpayers on the basis of U.S. or foreign stock ownership. Eligibility for the exception to the tax on liquidating distributions for distributions to non-exempt, U.S. corporate parents is not based upon the nationality of the owners of the distributing corporation, but rather is based upon whether such owners would be subject to corporate tax if they subsequently sold or distributed the same property. Thus, the exception does not apply to distributions to persons that would not be so subject -- not only foreign corporations, but also tax-exempt organizations. A similar analysis applies to the treatment of section 355 distributions subject to section 367(e)(1).

For the reasons given above in connection with the discussion of paragraph 2 of the Article, it is also understood that the provision in section 1446 of the Code for withholding of tax on non-U.S. partners does not violate paragraph 4 of the Article.

It is further understood that the ineligibility of a U.S. corporation with nonresident alien shareholders to make an election to be an "S" corporation does not violate paragraph 4 of the Article. If a corporation elects to be an S corporation (requiring 35 or fewer shareholders), it is generally not subject to income tax and the shareholders take into account their pro rata shares of the corporation's items of income, loss, deduction or credit. (The purpose of the provision is to allow an individual or small group of individuals to conduct business in corporate form while paying taxes at individual rates as if the business were conducted directly.) A nonresident alien does not pay U.S. tax on a net basis, and, thus, does not generally take into account items of loss, deduction or credit. Thus, the S corporation provisions do not exclude corporations with nonresident alien shareholders because such shareholders are foreign, but only because they are not net-basis taxpayers. Similarly, the provisions exclude corporations with other types of shareholders where the purpose of the provisions cannot be fulfilled or their mechanics implemented. For example, corporations with corporate shareholders are excluded because the purpose of the provisions to permit individuals to conduct a business in corporate form at individual tax rates would not be furthered by their inclusion.

*Paragraph 5*

Paragraph 5 of the Article confirms that no provision of the Article will prevent either Contracting State from imposing the branch tax described in paragraph 8 of Article 10 (Dividends). Since imposition of the branch tax under the Convention is specifically sanctioned by paragraph 8 of Article 10 (Dividends), its imposition could not be precluded by Article 25, even without paragraph 5. Under the generally accepted rule of construction that the specific takes precedence over the more general, the specific branch tax provision of Article 10 would take precedence over the more general national treatment provision of Article 25.

*Relation to Other Articles*

The saving clause of paragraph 4 of Article 1 (General Scope) does not apply to this Article, by virtue of the exceptions in paragraph 5(a) of Article 1. Thus, for example, a U.S. citizen who is a resident of Ireland may claim benefits in the United States under this Article.

Nationals of a Contracting State may claim the benefits of paragraph 1 regardless of whether they are entitled to benefits under Article 23 (Limitation on Benefits), because that paragraph applies to nationals and not residents. They may not claim the benefits of the other paragraphs of this Article with respect to an item of income unless they are generally entitled to treaty benefits with respect to that income under a provision of Article 23.


## Article 26 (Mutual Agreement Procedure)

This Article provides the mechanism for taxpayers to bring to the attention of competent authorities issues and problems that may arise under the Convention. It also provides a mechanism for cooperation between the competent authorities of the Contracting States to resolve disputes and clarify issues that may arise under the Convention and to resolve cases of double taxation not provided for in the Convention. The Article also provides for the possibility of the use of arbitration to resolve disputes that cannot be settled by the competent authorities. The competent authorities of the two Contracting States are identified in paragraph 1(e) of Article 3 (General Definitions).

*Paragraph 1*

This paragraph provides that where a resident of a Contracting State considers that the actions of one or both Contracting States will result in taxation that is not in accordance with the Convention he may present his case to the competent authority of either Contracting State. Nearly all U.S. treaties allow taxpayers to bring competent authority cases only to the competent authority of their country of residence, or citizenship/nationality. Paragraph 16 of the OECD Commentary to Article 26 suggests, however, that countries may agree to allow a case to be brought to either competent authority. Because there seems to be no apparent reason why a resident of a Contracting State must take its case to the competent authority of its State of residence and not to that of the partner, the Convention, like the U.S. Model, adopts the approach suggested in the OECD Commentary. Under this approach, a U.S. permanent establishment of a corporation resident in the treaty partner that faces inconsistent treatment in the two countries would be able to bring its complaint to the competent authority in either Contracting State.

Although the typical cases brought under this paragraph will involve economic double taxation arising from transfer pricing adjustments, the scope of this paragraph is not limited to such cases. For example, if a Contracting State treats income derived by a company resident in the other Contracting State as attributable to a permanent establishment in the first-mentioned Contracting State, and the resident believes that the income is not attributable to a permanent establishment, or that no permanent establishment exists, the resident may bring a complaint under paragraph 1 to the competent authority of either Contracting State.

It is not necessary for a person bringing a complaint first to have exhausted the remedies provided under the national laws of the Contracting States before presenting a case to the competent authorities, nor does the fact that the statute of limitations may have passed for seeking a refund preclude bringing a case to the competent authority. Like the U.S. Model, but unlike the OECD Model, no time limit is provided within which a case must be brought.

*Paragraph 2*

This paragraph instructs the competent authorities in dealing with cases brought by taxpayers under paragraph 1. It provides that if the competent authority of the Contracting State to which the case is presented judges the case to have merit, and cannot reach a unilateral solution, it shall seek an agreement with the competent authority of the other Contracting State pursuant to which taxation not in accordance with the Convention will be avoided. Any agreement is to be implemented even if such implementation otherwise would be barred by the statute of limitations or by some other procedural limitation, such as a closing agreement. In a case where the taxpayer has entered a closing agreement (or other written settlement) with the United States prior to bringing a case to the competent authorities, the U.S. competent authority will endeavor only to obtain a correlative adjustment from Ireland. See, Rev. Proc. 96-13, 1996-3 I.R.B. 31, section 7.05. Because, as specified in paragraph 2 of Article 1 (General Scope), the Convention cannot operate to increase a taxpayer's liability, time or other procedural limitations can be overridden only for the purpose of making refunds and not to impose additional tax.

*Paragraph 3*

Paragraph 3 authorizes the competent authorities to resolve difficulties or doubts that may arise as to the application or interpretation of the Convention. The paragraph includes a non-exhaustive list of examples of the kinds of matters about which the competent authorities may reach agreement. This list is purely illustrative; it does not grant any authority that is not implicitly present as a result of the introductory sentence of paragraph 3. The competent authorities may, for example, agree to the same attribution of income, deductions, credits or allowances between an enterprise in one Contracting State and its permanent establishment in the other (subparagraph (a)) or between related persons (subparagraph (b)). These allocations are to be made in accordance with the arm's length principle underlying Article 7 (Business Profits) and Article 9 (Associated Enterprises). Agreements reached under these subparagraphs may include agreement on a methodology for determining an appropriate transfer price, common treatment of a taxpayer's cost sharing arrangement, or upon an acceptable range of results under that methodology. Subparagraph (h) makes clear that they may also agree to apply this methodology and range of results prospectively to future transactions and time periods pursuant to advance pricing agreements.

As indicated in subparagraphs (c), (d), (e) and (f), the competent authorities also may agree to settle a variety of conflicting applications of the Convention. They may agree to characterize particular items of income in the same way (subparagraph (c)), to characterize entities in a particular way (subparagraph (d)), to apply the same source rules to particular items of income (subparagraph (e)), and to adopt a common meaning of a term (subparagraph f)).

Subparagraph (g) authorizes the competent authorities to increase any dollar amounts referred to in the Convention to reflect economic and monetary developments. Under the Convention, this refers only to Article 17 (Artistes and Sportsmen). The rule under paragraph (h) is intended to operate as follows: if, for example, after the Convention has been in force for some time, inflation rates have been such as to make the $20,000 exemption threshold for entertainers unrealistically low in terms of the original objectives intended in setting the threshold, the competent authorities may agree to a higher threshold without the need for formal amendment to the treaty and ratification by the Contracting States. This authority can be exercised, however, only to the extent necessary to restore those original objectives. Because of paragraph 2 of Article 1 (General Scope), it is clear that this provision can be applied only to the benefit of taxpayers, i.e., only to increase thresholds, not to reduce them.

Subparagraph (i) makes clear that the competent authorities can agree to the common application, consistent with the objective of avoiding double taxation, of procedural provisions of the internal laws of the Contracting States, including those regarding penalties, fines and interest.

Since the list under paragraph 3 is not exhaustive, the competent authorities may reach agreement on issues not enumerated in paragraph 3 if necessary to avoid double taxation. For example, the competent authorities may seek agreement on a uniform set of standards for the use of exchange rates, or agree on consistent timing of gain recognition with respect to a transaction to the extent necessary to avoid double taxation.

Finally, paragraph 3 authorizes the competent authorities to consult for the purpose of eliminating double taxation in cases not provided for in the Convention and to resolve any difficulties or doubts arising as to the interpretation or application of the Convention. This provision is intended to permit the competent authorities to implement the treaty in particular cases in a manner that is consistent with its expressed general purposes. It permits the competent authorities to deal with cases that are within the spirit of the provisions but that are not specifically covered. An example of such a case might be double taxation arising from a transfer pricing adjustment between two permanent establishments of a third-country resident, one in the United States and one in Ireland. Since no resident of a Contracting State is involved in the case, the Convention does not apply, but the competent authorities nevertheless may use the authority of the Convention to prevent the double taxation. Ireland requested a mutual understanding (paragraph 5 of the Diplomatic Notes) that this provision applies only with respect to covered taxes.

Agreements reached by the competent authorities under paragraph 3 need not conform to the internal law provisions of either Contracting State. Paragraph 3 is not, however, intended to authorize the competent authorities to resolve problems of major policy significance that normally would be the subject of negotiations between the Contracting States themselves. For example, this provision would not authorize the competent authorities to agree to allow a U.S. foreign tax credit under the treaty for a tax imposed by the other country where that tax is not otherwise a covered tax and is not an identical or substantially similar tax imposed after the date of signature of the Convention. In such a case, the creditability of the tax would be determined under the Code and regulations.

Paragraph 3 also requires the competent authorities of both Contracting States to publish any principle of general application established by agreement or agreements of the competent authorities. This provision is not contained in the U.S. Model, but it is the practice of the U.S. competent authority to publish agreements reached under any convention that have broad application.

*Paragraph 4*

Paragraph 4 provides that the competent authorities may communicate with each other for the purpose of reaching an agreement. This makes clear that the competent authorities of the two Contracting States may communicate without going through diplomatic channels. Such communication may be in various forms, including, where appropriate, through face-to-face meetings of the competent authorities or their representatives.

*Paragraph 5*

Paragraph 5 contains an arbitration procedure found in several recent U.S. tax treaties, although the arbitration procedures currently are operative only under the treaty with Germany. Paragraph 5 provides that where the competent authorities have been unable to resolve a disagreement regarding the application or interpretation of the Convention, the disagreement may, by mutual consent of the competent authorities and the affected taxpayers, be submitted for arbitration. Nothing in the provision requires that any case be submitted for arbitration. If a case is submitted to an arbitration board, however, the board's decision in that case will be binding on both Contracting States and the taxpayer(s) with respect to that case.

When a case is referred to an arbitration board, confidential information necessary for carrying out the arbitration procedure may be released by the States to the board. The members of the board, and any staff, however, are subject to the disclosure rules of Article 27.

The arbitration procedures will not come into effect until the Contracting States have agreed through an exchange of diplomatic notes. It is anticipated that the two States will consider exchanging diplomatic notes implementing the arbitration procedure at such time the provisions under the other Conventions, and the European Communities agreement signed on 23 July, 1990, prove satisfactory to the competent authorities of both the United States and Ireland. The arbitration procedures themselves also will be established through an exchange of notes.

*Other Issues*

*Treaty effective dates and termination in relation to competent authority dispute resolution*

A case may be raised by a taxpayer under a treaty with respect to a year for which a treaty was in force after the treaty has been terminated. In such a case the ability of the competent authorities to act is limited. They may not exchange confidential information, nor may they reach a solution that varies from that specified in its law.

A case also may be brought to a competent authority under a treaty that is in force, but with respect to a year prior to the entry into force of the treaty. The scope of the competent authorities to address such a case is not constrained by the fact that the treaty was not in force when the transactions at issue occurred, and the competent authorities have available to them the full range of remedies afforded under this Article.

*Triangular competent authority solutions*

International tax cases may involve more than two taxing jurisdictions (e.g., transactions among a parent corporation resident in country A and its subsidiaries resident in countries B and C). As long as there is a complete network of treaties among the three countries, it should be possible, under the full combination of bilateral authorities, for the competent authorities of the three States to work together on a three-sided solution. Although country A may not be able to give information received under Article 27 (Exchange of Information and Administrative Assistance) from country B to the authorities of country C, if the competent authorities of the three countries are working together, it should not be a problem for them to arrange for the authorities of country B to give the necessary information directly to the tax authorities of country C, as well as to those of country A. Each bilateral part of the trilateral solution must, of course, not exceed the scope of the authority of the competent authorities under the relevant bilateral treaty.

*Relation to Other Articles*

This Article is not subject to the saving clause of paragraph 4 of Article 1 (General Scope) by virtue of the exceptions in paragraph 5(a) of that Article. Thus, rules, definitions, procedures, etc. that are agreed upon by the competent authorities under this Article may be applied by the United States with respect to its citizens and residents even if they differ from the comparable Code provisions. Similarly, as indicated above, U.S. law may be overridden to provide refunds of tax to a U.S. citizen or resident under this Article. A person may seek relief under Article 26 regardless of whether he is generally entitled to benefits under Article 23 (Limitation on Benefits). As in all other cases, the competent authority is vested with the discretion to decide whether the claim for relief is justified.

## Article 27 (Exchange of Information and Administrative Assistance)

*Paragraph 1*

This Article provides for the exchange of information between the competent authorities of the Contracting States. The information to be exchanged is that which is relevant for carrying out the provisions of the Convention or the domestic laws of the United States or of Ireland concerning the taxes covered by the Convention. The OECD Model refers to information that is "necessary" for carrying out the provisions of the Convention, etc. This term consistently has been interpreted as being equivalent to "relevant," and as not requiring a requesting State to demonstrate that it would be disabled from enforcing its tax laws unless it obtained a particular item of information. To remove any potential misimpression that the term "necessary" created a higher threshold than relevance, the Convention, like the U.S. Model, adopts the term "relevant."

Exchange of information with respect to domestic law is authorized insofar as the taxation under those domestic laws is not contrary to the Convention. Thus, for example, information may be exchanged with respect to a covered tax, even if the transaction to which the information relates is a purely domestic transaction in the requesting State and, therefore, the exchange is not made for the purpose of carrying out the Convention. An example of such a case is provided in the OECD Commentary: A company resident in the United States and a company resident in the partner transact business between themselves through a third-country resident company. Neither Contracting State has a treaty with the third State. In order to enforce their internal laws with respect to transactions of their residents with the third-country company (since there is no relevant treaty in force), the Contracting State may exchange information regarding the prices that their residents paid in their transactions with the third-country resident. However, unlike the U.S. Model, the Convention does not extend exchange of information beyond the covered taxes in Article 2 because of restrictions under Irish law.

Paragraph 1 states that information exchange is not restricted by Article 1 (General Scope). Accordingly, information may be requested and provided under this Article with respect to persons who are not residents of either Contracting State. For example, if a third-country resident has a permanent establishment in Ireland which engages in transactions with a U.S. enterprise, the United States could request information with respect to that permanent establishment, even though it is not a resident of either Contracting State. Similarly, if a third--country resident maintains a bank account in Ireland, and the Internal Revenue Service has reason to believe that funds in that account should have been reported for U.S. tax purposes but have not been so reported, information can be requested from Ireland with respect to that person's account.

Paragraph 1 also provides assurances that any information exchanged will be treated as secret, subject to the same disclosure constraints as information obtained under the laws of the requesting State. Information received may be disclosed only to persons, including courts and administrative bodies, concerned with the assessment, collection, enforcement or prosecution in respect of the taxes to which the information relates, or to persons concerned with the administration of these taxes. The information must be used by these persons in connection with these designated functions. Persons in the United States concerned with the administration of taxes include legislative bodies, such as the tax-writing committees of Congress and the General Accounting Office. Information received by these bodies must be for use in the performance of their role in overseeing the administration of U.S. tax laws. Information received may be disclosed in public court proceedings or in judicial decisions.

The Article authorizes the competent authorities to exchange information on a routine basis, on request in relation to a specific case, or spontaneously. It is contemplated that the Contracting States will utilize this authority to engage in all of these forms of information exchange, as appropriate.

*Paragraph 2*

Paragraph 2 is identical to paragraph 2 of Article 26 of the OECD Model and paragraph 2 or Article 26 of the U.S. Model. It provides that the obligations undertaken in paragraph 1 to exchange information do not require a Contracting State to carry out administrative measures that are at variance with the laws or administrative practice of either State. Nor is a Contracting State required to supply information not obtainable under the laws or administrative practice of either State, or to disclose trade secrets or other information, the disclosure of which would be contrary to public policy. Thus, a requesting State cannot obtain information from the other State if the information would be obtained pursuant to procedures or measures that are broader than those available in the requesting State.

While paragraph 2 states conditions under which a Contracting State is not obligated to comply with a request from the other Contracting State for information, the requested State is not precluded from providing such information, and may, at its discretion, do so subject to the limitations of its internal law.

*Paragraph 3*

Paragraph 3 does not have an analog in the OECD Model. Paragraph 3 provides that when information is requested by a Contracting State in accordance with this Article, the other Contracting State is obligated to obtain the requested information as if the tax in question were the tax of the requested State, even if that State has no direct tax interest in the case to which the request relates. The OECD Model does not state explicitly in the Article that the requested State is obligated to respond to a request even if it does not have a direct tax interest in the information. The OECD Commentary, however, makes clear that this is to be understood as implicit in the OECD Model. (See paragraph 16 of the OECD Commentary to Article 27.) Although Ireland has not entered an observation to the Commentary on this point, paragraph 10 of the Protocol states that the laws and practices of Ireland currently do not permit it to obtain information in cases where it does not have a tax interest. However, if the laws and practices of Ireland change in this respect, Ireland will carry out enquiries on behalf of the United States in such cases.

The first sentence of paragraph 3 of the U.S. Model, which provides the authority to obtain and provide information from financial institutions, is not included in the Convention. However, paragraph 6 of the Diplomatic Notes accompanying the Convention and Protocol sets forth Ireland's agreement that the United States may, pursuant to a request under the provisions of the Irish Criminal Justice Act, 1994 (or any successor law), obtain information of financial institutions and depositions of witnesses for the purpose of investigating or prosecuting criminal fiscal offenses. The Irish negotiators confirmed that such requests may be made to the Irish Minister of Justice by the Department of Justice or the Internal Revenue Service.

Paragraph 3 further provides that the requesting State may specify the form in which information is to be provided (e.g., depositions of witnesses and authenticated copies of original documents) so that the information can be usable in the judicial proceedings of the requesting State. The requested State should, if possible, provide the information in the form requested to the same extent that it can obtain information in that form under its own laws and administrative practices with respect to its own taxes. In addition, Paragraph 6 of the diplomatic notes sets forth Ireland's agreement that the United States may, pursuant to a request under the provisions of the Irish Criminal Justice Act, 1994 (or any successor law), obtain information of financial institutions and depositions of witnesses for the purpose of the investigation of criminal fiscal offenses. Such requests may be made whether the investigation is undertaken by the Department of Justice or the Internal Revenue Service.

*Paragraph 4*

Finally, paragraph 4 provides that the competent authority of the requested State shall allow representatives of the applicant State to enter the requested State to interview individuals and examine a person's books and records with that individual's or person's consent.

A tax administration may seek information with respect to a year for which a treaty was in force after the treaty has been terminated. In such a case the ability of the other tax administration to act is limited. The treaty no longer provides authority for the tax administrations to exchange confidential information. They may only exchange information pursuant to domestic law.

The competent authority also may seek information under a treaty that is in force, but with respect to a year prior to the entry into force of the treaty. The scope of the competent authorities to address such a case is not constrained by the fact that a treaty was not in force when the transactions at issue occurred, and the competent authorities have available to them the full range of information exchange provisions afforded under this Article. Where a prior treaty was in effect during the years in which the transaction at issue occurred, the exchange of information provisions of the current treaty apply.

## Article 28 (Diplomatic Agents and Consular Officers)

This Article confirms that any fiscal privileges to which diplomatic or consular officials are entitled under general provisions of international law or under special agreements will apply notwithstanding any provisions to the contrary in the Convention. The text of this Article is identical to the corresponding provision of the U.S. and OECD Models. The agreements referred to include any bilateral agreements, such as consular conventions, that affect the taxation of diplomats and consular officials and any multilateral agreements dealing with these issues, such as the Vienna Convention on Diplomatic Relations and the Vienna Convention on Consular Relations. The U.S. generally adheres to the latter because its terms are consistent with customary international law.

The Article does not independently provide any benefits to diplomatic agents and consular officers. Article 19 (Government Service) does so, as do Code section 893 and a number of bilateral and multilateral agreements. Rather, the Article specifically reconfirms in this context the statement in paragraph 2 of Article 1 (General Scope) that nothing in the tax treaty will operate to restrict any benefit accorded by the general rules of international law or with any of the other agreements referred to above. In the event that there is a conflict between the tax treaty and international law or such other treaties, under which the diplomatic agent or consular official is entitled to greater benefits under the latter, the latter laws or agreements shall have precedence. Conversely, if the tax treaty confers a greater benefit than another agreement, the affected person could claim the benefit of the tax treaty.

Pursuant to subparagraph 5(b) of Article 1, the saving clause of paragraph 4 of Article 1 (General Scope) does not apply to override any benefits of this Article available to an individual who is neither a citizen of the United States nor has immigrant status there.

## Article 29 (Entry into Force)

This Article contains the rules for bringing the Convention into force and giving effect to its provisions.

*Paragraph 1*

Paragraph 1 provides for the ratification of the Convention by both Contracting States according to their constitutional and statutory requirements and requires that instruments of ratification be exchanged as soon as possible.

In the United States, the process leading to ratification and entry into force is as follows: Once a treaty has been signed by authorized representatives of the two Contracting States, the Department of State sends the treaty to the President who formally transmits it to the Senate for its advice and consent to ratification, which requires approval by two-thirds of the Senators present and voting. Prior to this vote, however, it generally has been the practice for the Senate Committee on Foreign Relations to hold hearings on the treaty and make a recommendation regarding its approval to the full Senate. Both Government and private sector witnesses may testify at these hearings. After receiving the advice and consent of the Senate to ratification, the treaty is returned to the President for his signature on the ratification document. The President's signature on the document completes the process in the United States.

*Paragraph 2*

Paragraph 2 provides that the Convention will enter into force upon the exchange of instruments of ratification. The date on which a treaty enters into force is not necessarily the date on which its provisions take effect. Paragraph 2, therefore, also contains rules that determine when the provisions of the treaty will have effect. Under paragraph 2(a), the Convention will have effect with respect to taxes withheld at source (principally dividends, interest and royalties) for amounts paid or credited on or after the first day of January next following the date on which the Convention enters into force. For example, if instruments of ratification are exchanged on April 25 of a given year, the withholding rates specified in paragraph 2 of Article 10 (Dividends) would be applicable to any dividends paid or credited on or after January 1 of the next year.

For all other taxes, paragraph 2(b) specifies that the Convention will have effect, in the case of United States taxes, for taxable years beginning on or after January 1 of the year following entry into force and, in the case of Irish taxes, for financial years (in the case of the corporation tax) or years of assessment (in the case of income tax and capital gains tax) beginning on or after January 1 of the year following entry into force. Because the federal excise tax on insurance premiums is collected quarterly and is not a withholding tax, the effective date provided by paragraph 2(b) will apply to that tax.

As discussed under Articles 25 (Mutual Agreement Procedure) and 26 (Exchange of Information), the powers afforded the competent authority under these articles apply retroactively to taxable periods preceding entry into force.

*Paragraph 3*

As in many recent U.S. treaties, Paragraph 3 provides a "grace period" in the form of a general exception to the effective date rules of paragraph 2. Under this paragraph, if the prior Convention would have afforded greater relief from tax to a person entitled to its benefits than would be the case under this Convention, that person may elect to remain subject to all of the provisions of the prior Convention for a twelve-month period from the date on which this Convention would have had effect under the provisions of paragraph 2 of this Article. During the period in which the election is in effect, the provisions of the prior Convention will continue to apply only insofar as they applied prior to the entry into force of the Convention.

For example, under the Convention a non-publicly traded corporation resident in Ireland that is wholly owned by third-country residents and that earns portfolio dividends from passive investments in the United States would be denied U.S. treaty benefits with respect to those dividends under the provisions of Article 23 (Limitation on Benefits). Since the prior Convention contained no anti-treaty-shopping rule, so that the corporation would be entitled to the reduced U.S. withholding rate of 15 percent, this corporation may elect under the grace period rule to be subject to the rules of the prior Convention for one additional year from the effective date specified in paragraph 2(a), thereby receiving U.S. treaty benefits for that period. This rule gives those residents of a Contracting State that are subject to the Limitation on Benefits provision an additional year to restructure their activities in a manner that would entitle them to qualify for benefits. Under the prior Convention, foreign source income attributable to a U.S. permanent establishment was not subject to U.S. tax. If an Irish resident has a U.S. permanent establishment that earns Canadian source income, that income would be exempt under the prior Convention, but taxable under the Convention. The Irish resident claiming that the Canadian-source income is exempt may do so for one additional year after the first taxable year beginning on or after the first day of January following entry into force of the new treaty.

If the grace period is elected, all of the provisions of the prior Convention must be applied for that additional year. The taxpayer may not apply certain, more favorable, provisions of the prior Convention and, at the same time, apply other, more favorable, provisions of the Convention. Thus, an Irish enterprise with a permanent establishment in the United States cannot rely on the prior Convention to avoid the branch profits tax and at the same time claim exemption from the branch level interest tax on excess interest on the basis that Article 11 (Interest) of the Convention eliminates source-basis taxation of interest (and therefore the excess interest tax). The enterprise must choose one regime or the other.

*Paragraph 4*

Paragraph 4 provides a rule to coordinate the termination of the prior Convention with the effective dates of the new treaty. The prior Convention will cease to have effect when the provisions of this Convention take effect in accordance with paragraphs 2 and 3 of the Article. Thus, for a person not taking advantage of the election in paragraph 3, the prior Convention will cease to have effect at the time, on or after January 1 of the year following entry into force of the Convention, when the provisions of the new Convention first have effect. For persons electing the additional year of coverage of the prior Convention, the prior Convention will remain in effect for one additional year beyond the date specified in the preceding sentence.

*Paragraph 5*

Paragraph 5 includes an additional transition rule with respect to the "derivative benefits" requirement of subparagraph 5 b) of Article 23 (Limitation on Benefits). Under this transition rule, an Irish company that is claiming the benefits of the Convention on the basis that it is owned by residents of EU or NAFTA countries may do so without regard to whether its owners would be entitled to benefits equivalent to those available under the Convention. This transition rule is available for a period of two years from when the Convention otherwise would have effect under the provisions of paragraphs 2 and 3.

For example, assume an Irish company owns 50 percent of a U.S. company from which it receives interest and dividends. The Irish company in turn is owned 30 percent by an Irish publicly traded company and 70 percent by a Canadian company and meets the base erosion standard of subparagraph 5 a) ii) of Article 23. If instruments of ratification were exchanged on November 15, 1997, the Convention will enter into force generally on January 1, 1998. Under the prior Convention, the Irish company was subject to U.S. withholding tax at a rate of 15% on dividends paid by the U.S. company because it did not meet the 95 percent ownership threshold to receive the direct dividend rate. That rate is reduced to 5% under the Convention for direct dividends. Accordingly, the Irish company does not elect to extend the effective date of the Convention pursuant to paragraph 3. However, as of January 1, 2000, the Irish company will no longer receive the benefits of the Convention with respect to interest paid by the U.S. company, because the Convention between the United States and Canada provides for a positive rate of withholding tax on interest and therefore the requirements of paragraph 5 b) of Article 23 will not be met. If, on the other hand, the Irish company owns 100 percent of the U.S. company, so that it qualified for the 5% direct dividend rate under the prior Convention, the Irish company could elect to apply the prior Convention for an additional year, as described above, so that it would not come into effect generally until January 1, 1999. In that case, the Irish company would receive benefits with respect to interest until January 1, 2001.

## Article 30 (Termination)

The Convention is to remain in effect indefinitely unless terminated by one of the Contracting States in accordance with the provisions of Article 30. The Convention may be terminated at any time after five years from the date on which it enters into force. If notice of termination is given, the provisions of the Convention with respect to withholding at source will case to have effect for amounts paid or credited on or after the first of January next following the expiration of the six months' period of notice. For other taxes, the Convention will cease to have effect for taxable years beginning on or after the first day of January next following the expiration of the six months' period of notice, in the case of the United States, and, in the case of Ireland, the Convention will cease to have effect for financial years (in respect of the corporation tax) and for years of assessment (in respect of the income and capital gains tax) beginning, in each case, on or after the first of January next following the expiration of the six months' notice period.

A treaty performs certain specific and necessary functions regarding information exchange and mutual agreement. In the case of information exchange the Convention's function is to override confidentiality rules relating to taxpayer information. In the case of mutual agreement its function is to allow competent authorities to modify internal law in order to prevent double taxation and tax avoidance. With respect to the effective termination dates for these aspects of the Convention, therefore, if a Convention is terminated as of January 1 of a given year, no otherwise confidential information can be exchanged after that date, regardless of whether the Convention was in force for the taxable year to which the request relates. Similarly, no mutual agreement departing from internal law can be implemented after that date, regardless of the taxable year to which the agreement relates. Therefore, for the competent authorities to be allowed to exchange otherwise confidential information or to reach a mutual agreement that departs from internal law, a Convention must be in force at the time those actions are taken and any existing competent authority agreement ceases to apply.

Article 30 relates only to unilateral termination of the Convention by a Contracting State. Nothing in that Article should be construed as preventing the Contracting States from concluding a new bilateral agreement, subject to ratification, that supersedes, amends or terminates provisions of the Convention without the six-month notification period.

Customary international law observed by the United States and other countries, as reflected in the Vienna Convention on Treaties, allows termination by one Contracting State at any time in the event of a "material breach" of the agreement by the other Contracting State.